I0606126

Babette's Bread

TOUCHWOOD

Stories, Recipes, and the Fundamental Techniques of Artisan Bread

BABETTE FRANCES KOURELOS

TouchWood Editions

touchwoodeditions.com

Edited by Marial Shea

Proofread by Senica Maltese

Cover and interior design by Jazmin Welch

Recipe photography by DL Acken. Supplementary photo credits listed on page 269

CATALOGUING DATA AVAILABLE FROM LIBRARY AND ARCHIVES CANADA

ISBN 9781771514101 (hardcover)

ISBN 9781771514118 (electronic)

TouchWood Editions acknowledges that the land on which we live and work is within the traditional territories of the Lkwungen (Esquimalt and Songhees), Malahat, Pacheedaht, Scia'new, T'So̲u-ke and WSÁNEĆ (Pauquachin, Tsartlip, Tsawout, Tseycum) peoples.

We acknowledge the financial support of the Government of Canada through the Canada Book Fund and of the Province of British Columbia through the Book Publishing Tax Credit.

This book was produced using FSC®-certified, acid-free papers, processed chlorine free, and printed with soya-based inks.

Printed in China

28 27 26 25 24 1 2 3 4 5

This book is dedicated to
my husband, Vasili Kourelos,
my love and my best friend.
Thank you for believing in my
work and for your unwavering
support. And to my familia,
for teaching me the importance
of family, of sitting down to
dinner, and the joy of preparing
(and sharing) good food.

γειά στα χέρια σου

(Pronounced geia sta cheria sou and translated "bless your hands," this is a Greek blessing for the hands of a person who prepares food.)

PREFACE 1

INTRODUCTION 5

ESSENTIAL BREAD-BAKING TOOLS 11

INGREDIENTS 19

WHEAT FARMING & MILLING 27

BAKING STEPS 33

Straight Dough Breads (Direct Method) 61

Pre-Fermented Breads 81

Cold-Fermented Breads 105

Welcome to the Wild Yeast . . . Here There Be Micro-organisms 123

Sweet & Enriched Breads 151

Rye & Whole-Grain Breads 171

Rolls, Buns & Wraps 189

Boiled, Fried & Steamed Breads 203

Quick Breads 219

Breads for the Pantry 229

Old Bread 245

FOLLOW THE BREADCRUMBS 257

FINAL THOUGHTS & RECOMMENDATIONS 263

ACKNOWLEDGEMENTS 265

FURTHER READING 267

CONVERSION CHART 268

PHOTO CREDITS 269

INDEX 271

Preface

It was late in the afternoon when I finally arrived at the bakery nestled amongst the maple trees in Westford, Vermont. All was still and quiet—except for a large wood-fired oven merrily hissing and crackling away in one corner of the bakehouse. Despite the silence, there was a tranquil energy about the room, as though it had been bustling with activity just a short while earlier and had only ceased for a brief moment of rest and reflection.

The sweet, earthy aroma of flour, fire, and yeast permeated the room. After travelling for more than thirty-two hours, I was relieved to be met by the tranquility and warmth of the bakery. It felt welcoming and familiar—like visiting your grandparents' house. Like coming home.

"What's your name?" the baker asked with a heavy French accent. "Babette," I said. "Non, non—your real name," he insisted. "Babette," I ventured again. Then, smiling, he said, "Welcome, welcome!"

• • •

I was named Babette after the French chef in the Danish short story and film *Babette's Feast*. And as luck (or fate) would have it, I eventually found my way into the kitchen.

In many ways, my appreciation of food was influenced by my family and my upbringing. My ancestors travelled from Holland, Greece, Italy, Germany, and France to South Africa—taking with them the traditions and food stories of earlier generations. Food is powerful like that. It connects the past with the present, offering comfort even when many miles from home. It perpetuates the significance of heritage, tradition, and belonging. Food, flavours, places, and people are forever connected by the invisible ties of tradition.

I grew up listening to stories of my great-grandfather Paradeisios Michaletos. How he left Greece at the age of seventeen and travelled to South Africa by ship, working as the vessel's cook to pay his fare. About the struggles he faced as a young immigrant in a foreign land. About his resilience and determination and his eventual triumph in opening the Hellenic Hotel in Pretoria. And stories about my grandmother's life growing up on a farm in the semi-desert of the Karoo in the 1940s—

of kneading and baking buttermilk rusks with her mother and grandmother. These stories fuelled my imagination and helped shape my culinary identity.

My mother, Theodora, introduced my sisters and me to the wonders of the kitchen—teaching us to appreciate fresh, quality ingredients and to be mindful about food. As such, Twinkies®, Vienna sausages, instant coffee, and margarine were unheard of in our household. And we enjoyed our tea and coffee with full-fat milk, no sugar. On weekends and as a special treat, my mother would buy freshly baked bread from La Spiga, the local Italian bakery. Slices of crusty olive ciabatta or dark whole-grain loaves would often find their way into our Monday lunch boxes—the highlight of the week! Rainy days were synonymous with pancakes—the thin kind, mind!—an example of the Dutch influence on the South African culinary tradition. All our meals took place around the kitchen table. And whenever guests were expected, the house would soon be filled with the tantalizing aroma of slow-roasting lamb seasoned with rosemary and garlic and drenched in lemon and olive oil.

I remember watching my father, Johan, prepare the dough for roosterkoek (grill cakes), which would later be baked over hot hardwood coals and enjoyed with ice-cold butter and perfectly grilled snoek (fish). And the care my sisters (Katharina and Frances) and I took in preparing stacks of braaibroodjies (sandwiches grilled over a fire), always buttering the bread on both sides! Breakfasts often consisted of "brood met kaas en koffie" (bread with cheese and coffee), and a new game of γιάντες / giántes (a very old Greek children's game) would always begin after a simple meal of roast chicken and the breaking of the wishbone.

The extended family often gathered for Sunday lunch at my Uncle Pedro's hotel, the Farm Inn in Pretoria, where magnificent buffet tables were stacked high with breads, salads, stews, and roasted meats. I always looked forward to those lunches, though more often than not my eyes proved bigger than my stomach!

My husband, Vasili, is Greek and our union has given me the opportunity to further explore my own Greek heritage. I am thankful for my mother-in-law, Melpo, who welcomed me into her kitchen and generously shares her recipes and culinary wisdom. With her help, I am slowly expanding my repertoire of Greek dishes and rediscovering the food traditions of my ancestors.

Now, based in beautiful Vancouver, I am adding a new chapter to an ongoing and multi-generational journey. New foods and different flavours are finding their way into our household, adding colour and zest to our lives. Yet, on difficult days, when the clouds gather and nostalgia and homesickness set in, I still seek the familiar comfort and reassurance of warm pancakes, homemade bread, and buttermilk rusks.

Introduction

Recipes evolve out of necessity, circumstance, and tradition. Out of scarcity and out of abundance. They are an eternal reflection of who we are, where we come from, and the times we have weathered. At the root of our shared culinary past lies bread, the humble carbohydrate and one of the very first foods made by our ancestors.

Bread embodies community, hospitality, and generosity. It is the ultimate comfort food, offering simple, satiating sustenance. It can be dressed up with fancy toppings or stuffed with a variety of tasty fillings. A loaf of bread can be used as a bowl, a plate, or to mop up beautiful gravies, hearty soups, and flavourful dressings. Even old bread can be refreshed or creatively repurposed. Yet, a really good bread can also stand on its own with little embellishment.

There is something magical, almost sacred about bread. The story of bread is closely entwined with the story of humanity, of struggle, perseverance, and triumph. Bread has stood the test of time; its significance is still deeply ingrained in our collective psyche today across cultures.

We work to earn our "bread and butter," we need "our daily bread" to survive, and we "break bread" with those closest to us on special and religious occasions. The allure and charm of bread is profound. We are instinctively drawn to it. It stirs primitive memories of self-sufficiency and survival but also of joy and abundance.

It is not surprising, then, that the Covid-19 pandemic of 2020 gave rise to an international bread-baking revolution. Instinctively, and almost overnight, everyone started baking bread! What may have started as a coping mechanism and an attempt to reduce widespread psychological stress soon became a reassuring and empowering pastime. While the world gasped for air, new life was being breathed into an age-old staple. Bread "rose" to the occasion (excuse the pun!). It offered us a much-needed support mechanism. Baking bread provided a sense of control and of purpose. It offered the comfort and community we so desperately craved, and quite literally became the staff of life once more. Bread captured the global imagination and reclaimed its place at the centre of our tables.

My own bread journey started in 2011, during the final two years of my law studies at the University of the Witwatersrand in Johannesburg, South Africa. Needing a creative outlet and a change of scenery from dry and tedious legal cases, I turned to baking. But my family soon had their fill of biscuits and sweet treats. On one particular afternoon, with the aroma of freshly baked oat crunchies still heavy in the air, my stepfather, Kevin, joined me at the kitchen table. He asked if I had considered baking anything other than cookies. Why not try to make something real, something basic, something one could eat all the time?

With his request in mind, I poured over my recipe books and eventually happened upon a recipe for a traditional English wholemeal cottage loaf. I was intrigued by its rather odd appearance—a small loaf sitting atop a larger one—and the idea of using honey as a sweetener instead of sugar. I studied the recipe and soon realized that I had found what I was looking for. After all, what could be more real or basic than bread?

Little did I know how that simple loaf of bread would forever change my life. That it would lead me away from a career in law and down an arguably harder but definitely more delicious and meaningful path. At some point during the mixing, shaping, and baking of that little loaf, something in me clicked. I fell in love with the simplicity and honesty of the entire process. I got my first taste of real bread and I was hungry for more!

So began my bread adventures. I would bake any and every bread recipe I could get my hands on. Soon I was baking so much bread that my mother stopped buying bread and her piano students were often sent home with a fresh loaf or two after their weekly music lessons.

And then the bread orders started coming in—from neighbours, friends, and acquaintances. I quickly realized that there was a growing market for good-quality artisan bread, but I did not yet feel accomplished enough to start a credible business. I felt that I needed formal training, an apprenticeship in a real bakery to truly hone my craft. But what would my mom have to say about me taking up baking instead of a career in law?

My worries were short lived. My mother quickly pointed out that, having completed my degrees, I could always fall back on law, should I ever want (or need) to. So, with her blessing, I started researching baking apprenticeships. By chance I stumbled on a blog post about a French baker in rural Vermont, in the US, who ran an apprenticeship program. The catch? He only took on apprentices with previous culinary training and was reachable only via old fashioned mail. So I wrote him a letter, explaining that though I did have a law degree, I was not a chef. I made a collage of all the breads I had baked and included it in my letter. Three weeks later, I received a call from the US. Had I really baked the loaves in the pictures? If so, I could start the apprenticeship.

Apprentice loaves

At the tender age of twenty-three, armed with a BA LLB and a newfound love of baking, I was off to America to apprentice under the late French Master Baker, Gérard Rubaud. At his bakery in Westford, Vermont, I learned the secrets of the levain (traditional French sourdough) and came to understand the workings of a wood-fired oven. It is there I perceived the true simplicity and essence of bread baking and realized that very little is required to create beautifully wholesome bread.

Gérard was old school. He did not allow cell phones or smart devices of any kind in the bakery. Imagine the horror! Everything was made out of wood (including the fermentation boxes). He had even made changes to his dough mixer so it would only run at one (very slow) speed. When there is no fancy modern equipment to speed up the process and do the work for you, you learn to read the dough. To develop your senses. To work with what you have and to adapt as necessary. "You have learned in three weeks what others learn in six months!" the baker announced while feeding the starter. Gérard devoted all his time and energy to the levain. And how truly exceptional his breads were—rustic, fragrant, and wholesome.

Gérard was then seventy-two years old. Having completed his apprenticeship in France at the age of thirteen, his relationship with bread was deeply ingrained, intuitive, almost spiritual. I am forever grateful for Gérard's tutelage and the practical experience I gained during my time in Vermont.

Upon returning to South Africa, I started baking from my mother's home in Doveton Road, Johannesburg. I set up a mailing list and invited our neighbours, my mother's students, and anyone who seemed interested in good bread to subscribe. I sent out weekly mailers letting customers know what and when I was baking, and people collected their breads from my mother's house.

The early days: My apprenticeship and baking from my mother's house.

Word of mouth did what it does best, and I soon outgrew the small home bakery and moved into a larger, more commercial kitchen in the heart of downtown Johannesburg's Maboneng Precinct, an area of urban renewal, home to many up-and-coming businesses. The double-volume bakery space boasted custom floor-to-ceiling windows and a viewing deck where patrons and passersby could observe the baking process or look down on the busy Johannesburg street below. From that small inner-city bakery I supplied many restaurants, coffee shops, and delicatessens with freshly baked artisan breads. The bakery also enjoyed loyal support from the immediate community and became a popular lunch destination. The "Gourmet Baguette" sandwich was a particular favourite of local artists and entrepreneurs, and we would sell out every day. Weekends were dedicated to bread workshops, where I would share my passion for bread with keen home bakers from all over South Africa.

The recipes in this book are the ones I turn to again and again—breads for the freezer, the pantry, and the kitchen counter. Honest bread. Basic bread. Daily bread. They are the breads I baked at my bakery in South Africa and the bread I bake for my family at home. Equipped with only a handful of basic ingredients and a simple understanding of fermentation, the home baker can produce wholesome and rustic breads—no fancy gadgets required.

This book is the culmination of years of learning: hands-on learning in my bakery, knowledge gained from baking for my family at home, and practical lessons learned during my weekly bread classes. After all these years of baking and teaching, I have gained insight into the most common problems and fears faced by home bakers. These recipes and baking techniques have grown out of that insight. I hope they will prove approachable, unintimidating, and, most importantly, enjoyable to novice and well-seasoned bread bakers alike.

This isn't a textbook. Rather, it is a collection of recipes for everyday life and everyday baking. A reliable guide for baking beautiful, real bread at home. I want to show you that baking bread is a simple process—simple enough to fit into your weekly or monthly schedule. In this book, you are guaranteed to find a bread that suits your palate and can comfortably slot into your schedule. Whether a simple sandwich loaf or the ever-elusive sourdough, there is a bread here to grab your attention and convince you to dust off your apron and get baking!

Happy baking always!
Babette

Babette's
Bread

Essential Bread-Baking Tools

When you are just starting out on your bread baking journey, it is easy to become overwhelmed by the variety of ingredients, utensils, and other gadgets that are available to home bakers. And with the Covid-19 pandemic giving rise to a global home-baking movement, there has been a great increase in articles pushing the latest "must have" and "must do" baking advice.

Over more than a decade of baking, I have definitely played with my fair share of baking tools and gadgets. So here follows an overview of my favourites, from the "nice to have" to the "cool but not 100 percent necessary." Ultimately, you can spend as little or as much as you want, but understand this: expensive trendy tools are not guaranteed to give you the best results. As long as you know how to understand, respect, and follow the principles and basic steps of the baking process, and give the dough the attention it needs, you can make do with the simplest, most inexpensive tools.

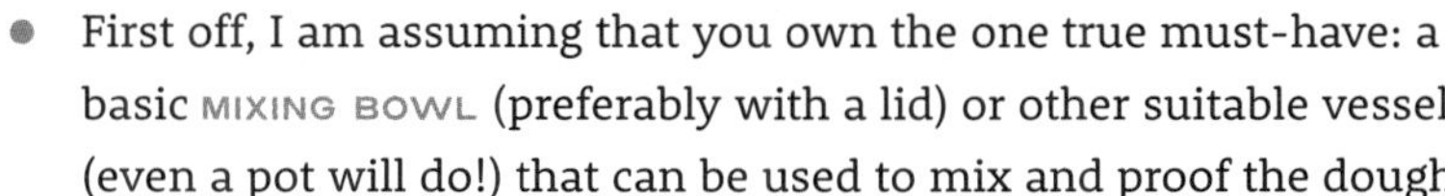

- First off, I am assuming that you own the one true must-have: a basic MIXING BOWL (preferably with a lid) or other suitable vessel (even a pot will do!) that can be used to mix and proof the dough.

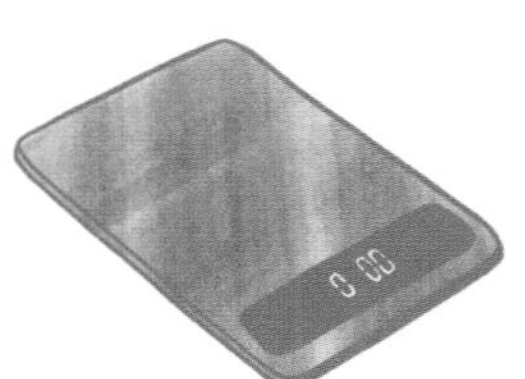

- For best results, I would also recommend having a SMALL KITCHEN SCALE so you can weigh your ingredients accurately. The recipes in this book are written using weight measurements first, followed by volume. (Ingredients are also listed in baker's percentages, a useful reference for more experienced bakers; see page 84 for more about this.) Once you start baking on a regular basis, I would strongly advise investing in a decent kitchen scale to improve the accuracy of your measurements and consistency of your bakes. Remember, though, the key is to get started and not wait until you have accumulated all the gear before you even attempt to bake your first loaf. So grab a mixing bowl or a pot and get stuck in without further delay.

- Now, let's talk about DOUGH SCRAPERS. This simple, unassuming, and wonderfully inexpensive little plastic tool will soon become your most trusted baking companion. When you are new to baking, everything feels awkward. You will be unsettled by the texture and stickiness of the dough. Tools will feel foreign and uncomfortable in your hands, including the dough scraper. But once you have baked a few loaves, you won't be able to mix a dough without it! (I am even considering keeping one in my handbag.)

  This magic little piece of plastic gives you the power to control even the unruliest of doughs. It allows you to effortlessly nudge the dough out of the bowl and onto your work surface; to scrape the sides of the mixing bowl; to remove stubborn bits of dough from your fingers and hands; to easily clean the countertop after the day's bake; and, last but not least, to fold, shift, lift, and transfer the dough with minimal effort. Dough scrapers come in all shapes and sizes. They can be made of hard or pliable plastic. You can opt for one with sharp or rounded edges. I prefer a combination. The sharp side can be used to cut/portion the dough (which is useful if you don't own a dough cutter) and the rounded edge can be used to mix the dough and scrape the sides of the mixing bowl.

- Next, I recommend using a FLOUR SHAKER. This nifty little tool can do so much more than flavour your popcorn or dust cinnamon or cocoa over your morning cappuccino. You are now going to use it to evenly distribute, or dust, flour onto your work surface. The flour shaker will allow you to control exactly how much flour you use to make the dough manageable. You don't want to add too much extra flour, as this will change the dough's texture and structure, and ultimately that of the final loaf. You may also inadvertently change the flavour of the dough (think salt-to-flour ratio and flavour balance).

Once you have portioned and shaped the pieces of dough, you can use the flour shaker to dust the bannetons (proofing baskets, see below) or couche (baker's proofing cloth) before resting the dough in/on them for a final rise. Furthermore, you may choose to apply a last dusting of flour before scoring and baking the dough. This tool isn't necessary on your first day of baking, but once you start making bread on a regular basis, the flour shaker will certainly make for an easier and more efficient shaping process. Your final loaves will acquire a more professional look, as they won't be covered in uneven clumps of flour.

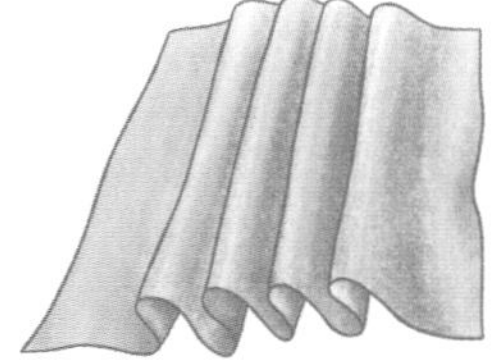

- The most traditional way to proof your shaped dough is in the soft (yet supportive) folds of fabric referred to as a baker's COUCHE. Usually, a large piece of thick linen is gathered into several folds (like a draped curtain). The shaped loaves are then lightly dusted with flour and placed within these folds, which offer enough gentle support for the dough to rise upwards instead of pancaking. You can also use a large kitchen towel (be sure to use one that is smooth textured so that the dough does not get stuck in the fibres) or a well floured bread basket/banneton. Once the loaves are nicely tucked in, loosely cover with a kitchen towel or fold the end of the couche over, to prevent them from developing a dry skin.

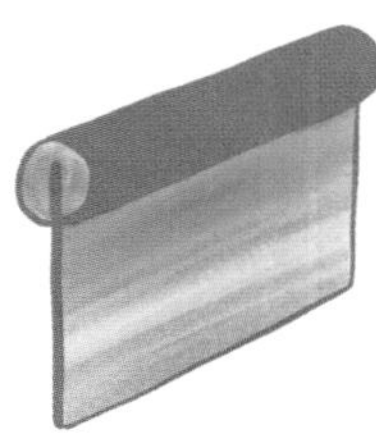

- The best tool for portioning or dividing the dough is the DOUGH CUTTER (a.k.a. BENCH SCRAPER). These stainless steel tools are available in various sizes with either a plastic or wooden handle. I have quite a collection and the oldest no longer has sharp edges. It is amazing what continuous use can do, even to metal!

  While you can use a sharp knife or even tear dough into pieces, a dough cutter will make your baking life just that little bit easier and less labour-intensive. In addition to smoothly cutting and portioning the dough, the bench scraper can be used to clean the countertop after shaping and working with the dough. It also comes in handy when you need to loosen a loaf from a baking sheet or pan. Interestingly, certain breads, like the Fougasse (page 111), are made by making very specific and deliberate cuts with the dough cutter.

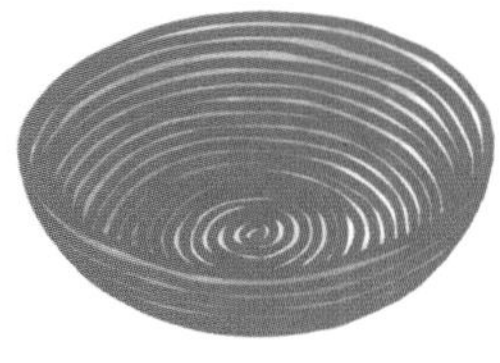

- Once you have a beautifully fermented dough, you will want to shape it and let it rest somewhere for the duration of the final rise prior to baking. A simple BANNETON or BREAD PROOFING BASKET will do the trick, but you *really* don't have to spend a fortune. Out of principle, I refuse to give in to the exorbitant price tags often attached to these simple cane baskets. Many home bakers fork out between twenty and fifty dollars because they are often showcased in baking books and online bread articles. The cane bannetons are popular because they allow you to achieve a beautiful spiral stencil on the finished loaf. If you are particularly keen on that look, and you are happy to pay the money, by all means, purchase away. But if, like me, you would rather spend that money on good baking ingredients, a new book, or seedlings for your vegetable garden, you have a couple of options:

If you don't want to spend any money at all, you can use a colander or any similar-sized bowl (lined with a flour-dusted dish towel). My favourite bread-proofing baskets are the woven baskets, commonly used in restaurants to serve bread at the beginning of a meal. They are simple, budget friendly, and easy to clean. These handwoven wicker or plastic baskets can be found at most kitchen or catering supply shops. Simply line them with a cloth napkin or cheesecloth, dust with flour, and put your shaped dough babies to bed. I particularly love the fact that you can get ten or more of these baskets for the price of a single cane banneton. But again, it is a matter of preference.

- Once your shaped dough has risen and is ready for the oven (finally!), you will need to score the surface of the dough before allowing it to face the heat. A very sharp kitchen knife, a pair of scissors, or a utility knife all work well. However, be careful, as the blade of the latter tends to rust. Professional bakers and avid home bakers use a **BAKER'S LAME**, **BAKER'S BLADE**, or **BREAD LAME**, which is essentially a handle (most often wooden or plastic) attached to an old-fashioned razor blade. The blade effortlessly slices through the outer skin of the dough and allows you to create practical, traditional, and/or decorative cuts. You can easily make your own or purchase one online—but do handle it with extreme care, as these blades can cause serious damage to your fingers!

- The secret to baking great bread in a domestic oven is twofold. You need very good, consistent heat and a whole lot of steam. On that note, not one oven is the same and thus it is important to get to know your oven—to read when the temperature needs to be increased or decreased to avoid underbaking or charring your precious loaf! For the steam, you can fill a deep oven tray with boiling water or ice cubes and place it on the lowest rack of the oven

Babette's bread
RASURKULTUR

or you can use a simple SPRAY BOTTLE to provide the necessary moisture for the dough to achieve the optimum oven spring. (Be advised that you will need to spray water into the oven regularly in the first twenty to twenty-five minutes.) The steam is necessary, as it prevents the crust from forming too quickly, thereby allowing the dough to rise to its full potential before the crust hardens and the final shape is achieved. A lack of steam will cause the crust to form before the dough has risen fully, which will in turn result in the trapped dough exploding in various directions (wherever there may be a weak spot in the dough or a flaw in your shaping technique), leaving you with lopsided and rather odd-looking bread. It will undoubtedly still be gloriously delicious, but the perfectionist in you (and in me) will want to do better.

- If the above methods sound a little too difficult or fiddly, you can also create the necessary steam by using any OVEN-SAFE POT (with handles that won't burn or melt and a dish that won't crack or shatter). Once the lid is on and sufficient heat has built up, the dough will create its own steam and easily rise to its full potential. There are some very fancy and rather expensive DUTCH OVENS on the market, but a cast iron or even enamel roaster can easily do the job and you will be churning out professional-looking loaves in no time! And if you have none of these at your disposal, you can place your dough on a baking sheet and turn a pot over it as a makeshift lid. Are you ready to bake yet?

- In choosing bread tins or loaf pans, ANY STANDARD-SIZE BREAD PAN will help you produce beautiful sandwich breads. However, a large PULLMAN PAN (with lid) is worth the investment if you are looking for consistent, uniform sandwich loaves.
- A selection of baking sheets of various sizes will also make a practical addition to your baking toolbox. As will a basic COOLING RACK to turn your piping-hot loaves onto as they come out of the oven and which will prevent the loaves from sweating and losing that wonderful crust.
- Lastly, a decent BREAD KNIFE (preferably long bladed and serrated) will come in handy—especially if you are baking on a regular basis and have developed a taste for a decent and decidedly robust crust.

Ingredients

Flour is flour, right? Wrong!

All flour is definitely not made equal. We need to look at this primary bread-baking ingredient in more detail. Not only do we have to differentiate between cake flour, bread flour, and all-purpose flour, we also have to consider the differences between commercial and artisanal flour (that is, bleached vs. unbleached and roller-milled vs. stone-ground flour). Not to mention organic flour, enriched flour, whole wheat, rye, and so on.

If we were to look inside most pantries around the world, we would probably find a bag of cake or all-purpose flour. These flours are perfectly suited for the occasional weekend or holiday bake. But not for a serious bread baker!

Recently however, another flour has become prevalent in our kitchens. I am, of course, referring to bread flour. As a result of the Covid-19 lockdowns, a bread-baking revolution unfolded. And with the help of social media, bread baking became one of the most talked about topics of 2020. When our survival instincts kicked in, flour became a hot, and very scarce, commodity. Bread, after all, has always been the staff of life. Suddenly, health concerns about gluten were the least of our problems and everyone scrambled to get their hands on the last available bags of flour. Even the folks who had never baked a single thing in their lives prior to the pandemic, now boasted well-stocked baking cupboards—but they had no idea where to start. I am guessing that many eventually took the leap and at least baked a handful of times. But for those of you who are still sitting on the baker's fence, hop on over and let me guide you through the first steps.

Typically, wheat flour is the most common flour used for bread baking. Bakers differentiate between different types of wheat flour by the protein content and the potential strength of the gluten that can be developed in doughs made with them. As a general rule, the higher the protein content, the stronger the resulting dough and its gluten structure is likely to be, which in turn yields loaves with good shape and volume (as opposed to a loaf pancaking due to insufficient flour/dough strength.) Flours are usually distinguished as cake flour, bread flour, all-purpose flour, whole-grain flour, and rye flour. Importantly, the same kinds of flour from different countries are not interchangeable because the average protein content for each type will vary from country to country. This variation is due to differences in wheat varieties, weather conditions, seasonal changes, and milling practices, giving flours unique water-absorbency levels, gluten strength, and coarseness. As such, you may need to change/tweak/adapt your recipes when baking in a new country, following a recipe from another country, or using a new brand of flour.

- CAKE FLOUR is made from soft wheat, which has the lowest protein content, and is usually milled very finely. Depending on the country of origin, the protein content may vary from 5 to 10 percent. The lower the protein content, the softer, lighter, and airier your baked goods will be. Due to its low protein content, this flour is not suitable for bread baking, as it is impossible to achieve a strong gluten structure, which means the dough cannot retain its shape (unless it is baked in a loaf tin).

- Next up, we have ALL-PURPOSE FLOUR. A perfect mix of soft and hard wheat, this flour is pretty versatile. With a protein content of 10 to 12 percent, it can form a decent gluten structure, making it well suited for bread baking. All-purpose flour (often shortened to AP) is commonly used in the United States and Canada, where it is the go-to flour for everyday baking. You can easily make your own all-purpose flour by mixing together equal amounts of cake and white bread flour.

- BREAD FLOUR usually has a protein content of 11 to 14 percent. Due to its high protein content, this flour can hold more water and produce a strong gluten structure, which allows the dough to easily retain its shape. The final loaf has good volume and yields a wonderfully chewy and open (bubbly) crumb.

  Remember that the protein percentage and overall performance of these flours may vary from country to country, and even from one bag to the next. Different wheat varieties, the age of the flour, unique climate and weather conditions, contrasting milling practices, the addition or lack of additives—these factors affect the character and constitution of the final product. In fact, the more natural and unadulterated the flour, the more likely you will find variances in the feel (texture) and behaviour of the flour (how the dough comes together, how much water it is able to absorb, etc.). Do not be unsettled by this. The more you bake, the more you will develop a feel for the dough and intuitively adapt to what each particular dough needs.

- WHOLEMEAL, WHOLE-GRAIN, WHOLE-WHEAT, and BROWN FLOURS contain varying amounts of the entire wheat kernel (wheat bran, wheat germ, and endosperm). The extraction percentages of these flours (what is removed from them during processing) differ from country to country. In some flours, both the wheat germ and the bran are removed prior to milling, with the bran milled back into the flour. Other

flours have a percentage of the wheat germ milled back into them. To gain better insight into the nature and composition of your flour, check the local legislation pertaining to flour milling (or talk to your local millers).

In any event, if you are looking to incorporate more whole grains into your diet, you can easily replace half the amount of white flour required in a recipe with the same amount of whole-grain flour. Whole-grain flour has a slightly darker colour (think brownish/tan) and coarser texture because of the presence of the wheat bran. Unlike baked goods made with pure white flour, those made with whole-grain flours will be a little more dense and heavy. This is because the bran is razor sharp and easily severs the delicate gluten strands, which severely weakens the dough structure and inhibits the size of the final loaf. However, rest assured that while you may be sacrificing volume, the final loaf is guaranteed to produce a tastier and more wholesome bread than a standard white loaf.

- Next we have RYE FLOUR. Rye falls within the wheat family but has a low *glutenin* content, which results in a lower *gluten* content in the dough and the final loaf. (Gluten is a full/complete protein formed out of the two partial proteins glutenin and gliadin.) People who suffer from gluten sensitivity may find it beneficial to favour rye bread over pure wheat breads. However, although lower in gluten, rye is definitely not gluten free. Also note that the three types of commercially available rye flours (light, medium, and dark) are named not for different varieties of rye, but for the amount of bran left in the flour. Thus, the darker the rye, the more whole grain the flour, while lighter flour is more refined. The texture of rye can be a bit intimidating if you are new to it—sticky and a little tricky to control. You may want to consider using a mix of 50 percent white flour and 50 percent rye instead of immediately tackling a 100 percent rye recipe. Although rye is considered by some to be an acquired taste, I believe the reason people think they do not enjoy rye is the common addition of caraway, cumin, or fennel seeds. You can easily omit these fragrant seeds and enjoy the natural taste of the rye instead.
- SEMOLINA FLOUR, with a protein content of about 13 percent or more, is a high-gluten flour. It is often used to make pasta as well as certain types of traditional breads and cakes, for example Greek Village Bread (page 143) or Italian Semolina Cakes. Known for its coarse texture and yellow colour, it is commonly used in Mediterranean baking and lends extra chewiness and a light sweetness to baked goods. This is a wonderful flour to add to your baking cupboard once you are ready to start adding other flours and textures to your breads.
- HERITAGE WHEATS, such as spelt, Red Fife, emmer, einkorn, and Kamut (to name only a few), are also becoming increasingly popular amongst artisan and home bakers who are keen to incorporate new ingredients with different characteristics and unique flavours into their bakes. The growing obsession with health food has put heritage grains and other ancient (non-wheat) grains such as quinoa, teff, buckwheat, sorghum, and amaranth in the spotlight. These days, it is quite common to find ancient grains in breads, crackers, and many other baked goods.

Other ingredients: salt, water, yeast, enrichments . . .

The other ingredients required to bake a simple yet wholesome loaf of bread are water, salt, yeast, and sometimes enrichments such as fats (butter/oil), dairy, eggs, or sugars. Each of these ingredients has a different impact on the fermentation process, the rising time, and the final loaf of bread.

Adding water is necessary to bring all the ingredients together to form a basic dough. Water also assists in the formation of gluten, as the partial proteins glutenin and gliadin bind through the addition of water to form the full protein, gluten. The temperature of the water added to a dough will vary from recipe to recipe and will need to be adjusted according to both the weather conditions on the baking day and the baker's specific intention for the dough.

On a cold day, it may be useful to use lukewarm water to help get the fermentation started and to encourage yeast activity by providing a suitable environment for the micro-organisms to come alive and flourish. Conversely, on a particularly hot day, it may be prudent to use cooler water when mixing the dough. This will help to slow down the fermentation and inhibit the yeast activity. It is important never to add boiling water to the dough, as it will scorch and severely weaken the yeast. (Some rye bread recipes call for scalding the rye flour prior to baking, which results in better structure and flavour in the final loaf. When preparing scalded rye bread, the yeast and other ingredients are only added once the scalded mixture has cooled off.)

Tap water, bottled water, mineral water, and sparkling water can all be used for bread baking. Water with a high mineral content (hard water) will decrease the yeast activity in the bread dough and should be boiled and left to cool prior to being used for baking. Other chemicals present in the water (such as chlorine) can also hamper yeast activity. Chlorinated water can be boiled or left in an uncovered container overnight and used to mix the dough the next day. Soft water, on the other hand, may increase the speed of fermentation and you may need to keep a closer eye on the dough.

Another crucial concept that goes hand in hand with water (and other liquids added to the dough) is hydration. Hydration refers to the ratio of water to flour in a given recipe. A lower hydration (less water) will yield a firmer dough, which will require kneading. A higher hydration (more liquid) will result in a wetter and softer dough, which will in turn require stretching and folding to build gluten strength as such wet doughs are impossible to knead.

For the dough to rise, it is necessary to add either fresh yeast, active dry yeast, instant yeast, or a refreshed sourdough culture into the mix. Always use the same type and quantity of yeast as the recipe calls for, as the above-mentioned types each react differently and cannot be used interchangeably.

Active dry yeast, for example, needs to be dissolved in water prior to being used. There is also a subtle difference in flavour between active dry and instant yeast. If you do not have the same yeast on hand as required in a recipe, you can do a quick Google search for a "yeast conversion table," which will show you how much yeast you should use. Alternatively, you may want to choose a recipe that calls for the type of yeast you do have. To accurately follow the recipes in this book, I recommend using instant dry yeast. For the sourdough loaves, you will need to make your own starter or obtain some from a friend or a friendly baker.

Yeast is a single-celled living organism. As soon as it is added to the dough, it will start to feed on the natural sugars in the flour (carbohydrates). The by-product of this feeding process is carbon dioxide, a gas that causes the dough to rise by filling the pockets created by the gluten network, blowing them up like small balloons. This digestion of the carbohydrates by the yeast also results in the production of alcohol and organic acids, which add flavour and character to the final loaf. This process is called fermentation.

Yeast activity can be controlled by adding a *specific* amount of yeast to the dough or by decreasing or increasing the ambient temperature and leaving the dough to rise in a colder or warmer environment. Note that using more yeast in a recipe will accelerate the rising of the dough and may also increase the yeasty flavour of the bread. However, make sure to keep a close eye on the dough to prevent it from over-fermenting. Conversely, adding less yeast will slow down fermentation and will require a longer rising time.

A longer, slower fermentation is especially beneficial, as it produces bread that is easier to digest (the dough has been pre-digested by the yeast and enzymes during the fermentation period). Breads that are allowed an extended fermentation time will taste better and boast richer colours and caramelization of the crust than loaves afforded only a short (and accelerated) rising time. Thus, by carefully monitoring the yeast activity and fermentation process, we are able to produce foods and beverages with wonderful flavour and digestive value. Fermentation is also a means of naturally preserving food and drinks without the need for artificial preservatives or chemical additives. In other words, the longer the dough is allowed to ferment (within controlled parameters) the longer it will naturally remain fresh and shelf stable.

Salt is included in the dough to enhance the flavour of the bread. In addition to slowing down the fermentation (as it inhibits yeast activity), salt also naturally improves the shelf life and final colour (crust) of baked goods. Do measure the salt accurately to achieve the best possible balance of flavour. If using coarse salt, dissolve it in a small amount of the water required in the recipe to avoid having crunchy bits in the final loaf. For the recipes in this book, I recommend using fine sea salt or table salt, though any other types will work just as well.

Enrichments such as fats, oils, eggs, dairy, and sugar produce soft, fluffy breads, but they slow the yeast activity, making a longer rising time necessary. More about this on page 151.

Wheat Farming & Milling

When I was a law student, one of my favourite subjects was consumer law. To this day—and despite the fact that my career has taken a different course—I remain passionate about consumer rights. I firmly support sharing food-production and food-labelling information with consumers; without access to honest, transparent information, consumers are neither able to enter into fair transactions nor make educated and informed purchasing decisions. The sharing of this information is particularly relevant today, given the growing number of people struggling with food-related sensitivities, allergies, and lifestyle diseases.

The information we need when baking or purchasing bread includes how the wheat was grown, harvested, and milled, and which (if any) additives are present in the flour or baked product. As a general rule (and if you are going to go to the trouble of baking your own bread), choose a flour that has been processed as little as possible, preferably stone-ground, unbleached, and containing few to no additives or preservatives–bonus if it is organic!

The Real Bread Campaign in the UK is doing groundbreaking work in holding manufacturers and producers to account and providing consumers with access to relevant information and education about their daily bread.

To provide useful and factual information about wheat flour (as the primary ingredient in bread baking), I reached out to various independent wheat farmers and artisanal millers in Canada and South Africa. They gave me greater insight into the production process of a humble bag of bread flour. Black Fox Flour (Canada), One Organic Farm (Canada), Eureka Mills (South Africa), and Champagne Valley Stonemill (South Africa) are like-minded and passionate producers intent on developing a community of informed and discerning bakers—in both domestic and commercial settings. And despite farming and milling in different provinces and on different continents, they share a common goal: to reintroduce us to the incredible flavours, aromas, and nutritional benefits of freshly milled, unadulterated flour.

To better understand the world of natural and freshly milled flours, it is helpful to first take a quick look at the commercial flour-production process. I would like to stress that this information is by no means intended to attack or vilify commercial flour or commercial milling practices, both of which play an integral role in large-scale food production and do a fantastic job in providing affordable staple foods to a global population. Nor is my aim to downplay the significance, usefulness, and advantages of these shelf-stable staple foods. However, as with most things in life, both the pros and the cons are worthy of consideration.

Due to competitive business practices and a global need for shelf-stable groceries, most commercial flour on retail shelves, has been stripped of both the wheat germ and bran. The grain used in the production of this flour is specifically grown to be milled by industrial roller mills as it allows for the efficient separation and extraction of the grain components (endosperm, germ, and bran) to produce shelf-stable white flour. This flour is often bleached using chemicals such as chlorine, bromic acid, and peroxide (though there does appear to be a movement away from bleaching and toward the optimization of the shape of the wheat kernel, to achieve a higher yield of the white starch.)

The wheat germ is oily by nature, giving it the tendency to go rancid (spoil), so it is removed from flour to extend its shelf life. The wheat bran is removed to produce a whiter, lighter, more refined flour. In short, all the natural goodness of the wheat has been lost and what is left is a bland and homogenous flour with very little nutritional value. To rectify this, commercial flour producers add artificial vitamins and minerals back into the flour. This is referred to as "fortification" or "enrichment." In some countries, the enrichment of flour is enforced by law. For example, in places where bread is an important staple food, fortification is often used as a means of improving access to essential micronutrients. However, some of the legislation pertaining to fortification is very old (dating back to the 1940s) and may require revision. Successfully spreading a concentrated amount of micronutrients into an industrial batch of flour is difficult, with some bags (and loaves) ending up with too much and others not any. And whether those micronutrients are in fact bioavailable is also questionable. For these reasons, it is unclear exactly how helpful and successful fortification really is.

At this point the flour in the commercial milling setting has already undergone quite significant changes, but it is then mixed with preservatives, sugars, colourants, stabilizers, dough conditioners, dough enhancers, and other additives that speed up or entirely eliminate the bulk fermentation time. This is good for business, but not so good for our digestion.

By contrast, the processes involved in the production of more natural flours (stone-ground, unbleached, organic, etc.) seem rather less radical. Independent and bespoke millers are selective about the type and quality of wheat they mill and try to support local and small-scale (or nonindustrial) wheat farmers who employ sustainable, regenerative, and/or organic farming practices. In short, an approach to farming that avoids the use of pesticides, herbicides, or fungicides and instead treats the soil as a biological system. These farming practices rely on no-till methods and crop rotation to reduce the need for harmful and invasive chemicals and encourage a symbiotic relationship within the living soil (earthworms and microbial life). This approach to farming promotes biodiversity and soil health instead of over-industrializing and chemicalizing the soil. Furthermore, the farmers are not subjected to harmful chemicals while farming (as happens when spraying crops with Roundup and glyphosate), and neither are consumers. It goes without saying that farming regeneratively (as well as organically) is more costly, but for these passionate farmers the rewards far outweigh the costs. These farms become generational assets that enrich the lives of whole communities.

Thus, natural and artisanal flours are milled (at least in theory) from quality grains that are free of GMOs and other additives. And in the case of organic flours, they should also not be subjected to fumigation or irradiation (measures that facilitate pest control and prevent food poisoning from harmful bacteria). When flour is milled the traditional and old-fashioned way, using millstones as opposed to high-speed rollers, more of the natural goodness of the grain remains unaltered. Stone milling does not reach the same high speeds or searing temperatures, which means that most of the nutrients remain intact and are not burned off. The millstones themselves are moulded from natural materials such as emery, flint, and magnesite and the milling involves gentle and slow processing of the grain.

In Canada, hard red spring wheat is usually milled into bread flour, whereas hard red winter wheat is used in South Africa. Hard wheat is high in protein and generally allows for much better gluten formation. In other words, it yields an elastic dough that can stretch, trap air, and hold its shape. Hard wheat is also capable of undergoing longer fermentation periods, which result in breads that are lower on the glycemic index and easier to digest. Soft wheat does not form gluten nearly as well and is better suited for use in baked goods that require a lighter (more delicate) structure such as cakes and pastries. During stone milling, the wheat berry is flaked, creating a larger surface area, which in turn allows for greater absorption of moisture during the bread-mixing process. Unsurprisingly, unbleached stone-ground flours are the flours of choice for most artisan bakers.

Furthermore, freshly milled natural and whole grain flours are more likely to contain the entire wheat kernel. In other words, they still have the wheat bran, endosperm, and wheat germ in the flour. The advantage of having all three components in the final flour is that bakers are able to produce breads that retain the natural goodness (vitamins, minerals, flavours, aromas, and fibre) of the grain. The exceptions are artisanal white bread and cake flours, which have a large portion of the bran removed (but should still contain the wheat germ). Again, when in doubt, it is always worth checking with the miller or retailer, as the rate of extraction (or inclusion) will vary from brand to brand and country to country. As these flours generally do not contain preservatives, they have a shorter shelf life. This puts additional pressure on an already competitive and ruthless business environment (especially for small businesses and small-scale producers), as many retailers require a minimum of six months shelf life.

Notwithstanding the challenges in producing simple, wholesome, unadulterated flour, these producers are making it possible for everyday consumers to rediscover old-fashioned flour, the way it was traditionally made, in addition to introducing them to a variety of ancient and heritage grains that are being resurrected by bold and adventurous farmers. As the Belgian Food Innovation Company, Puratos, so aptly states, "The future of bread lies in its past."

Thus, through the collective efforts of farmers, millers, bakers, and consumers, a new value chain is being established. A *real flour* and *real bread* culture is gaining momentum, and more and more artisan millers are finding their stone-milled, unbleached, and additive-free flour in high demand. And in places where there is a shortage of natural flours, bakers are opting to mill their own whole grains to supplement the refined flours that are more readily available.

But despite the myriad of nutritional and digestive benefits, premium artisan flour comes with a hefty price tag—one that inevitably will not be accessible to a large portion of consumers. This does not have to mean that the enjoyment of these ingredients is entirely out of reach. In fact, there are fantastic options available to home bakers that are guaranteed to suit most every budget.

Firstly, baking bread at home (even with commercial flour) is already significantly healthier and more nourishing than most supermarket loaves will ever be. Secondly, by adding wheat germ or supplementing a portion of the more refined white flour with freshly milled whole-grain flour, the home baker can quickly improve the nutritional and digestive value of the final baked product. And lastly, wheat berries (whole grains) can easily be milled at home on a small scale in a coffee or spice grinder, in some types of blenders (food processors), or in small countertop mills. Alternatively, these grains can be soaked in water overnight and mixed into a bread dough the following day, adding fibre, texture, and flavour to a simple homemade loaf.

> **"Is this flour enriched?" the health inspector asks, pointing at the large brown paper bags of flour piled high in one corner of the bakery. "No," I reply. "It doesn't need—" "It is required by law," she says while making a note of something on her list. "But this flour is natural," I venture. "It still contains all of its goodness. Nothing has been removed. Nothing has been extracted. It does not need fortification." She looks at the flour, and then at me, before signing the document in silence.**

Baking Steps

As with most undertakings in life, your baking success will require a solid plan (with steps) and a clear vision or goal of what you want to achieve. This requires precision, patience, and lots of practice. Just as you had to learn to crawl before you learned to walk, you will need to learn the basic steps of bread baking before you can start experimenting and veering from the tried and tested recipes. But if you are willing to put your shoulder into it (haha!), to learn the basics, and to eat humble pie for a while, you will slowly start to improve and eventually master the art of bread baking. Here are my ten steps to guide you along your baking journey.

1 Sourcing ingredients

This is not usually included as a step in the bread-baking process, and that is a pity in my opinion. The quality and type of ingredients you use have a great impact on the overall health benefits, quality, and flavour of the final product. This step is important because *you* get to source the ingredients that best suit your budget and are aligned with your health and wellness goals. Whether you hope to incorporate more whole grains and whole foods into your diet or reduce your intake of refined sugars or other highly processed ingredients, you have so many wonderfully wholesome options to have fun with. It doesn't have to be expensive either. You can bake gloriously simple yet nourishing bread on a tight budget. So have a good look at your baking cupboard. Let go of items you haven't used in months (or years!), get rid of (or donate) ingredients that no longer form part of your health and dietary vision, and begin to actively source ingredients you are happy to put into your body. Being more deliberate with your choice of ingredients will give you the extra reassurance of knowing exactly what you and your family are eating.

2 Creating a pre-ferment, refreshing your sourdough starter, and mixing an autolyse

Although it is definitely possible to bake a delicious and very nutritious loaf of bread without using a pre-ferment or sourdough starter (think a slow-fermented straight-dough country bread or a cold-fermented ciabatta), a pre-ferment and/or starter can add some serious depth of flavour and character to your bakes. Pre-ferments have the added benefit of acting as a natural preservative and also result in breads that are easy to digest due to the extended fermentation period.

Making a pre-ferment involves mixing a small amount of flour with water and a little bit of yeast or sourdough culture and allowing the mixture to develop for a few hours or overnight. This fermented mixture is then added to a new dough, which is then again left to ferment, develop, and rise before being shaped and baked.

If a recipe calls for a pre-ferment, don't skip over or rush this part because it sounds like an unnecessary and inconvenient step. If you really are pressed for time, look for a recipe that doesn't require a pre-ferment. (See straight dough loaves, page 61, or quick breads, page 219.)

When it comes to your sourdough starter, it is important to understand the processes of feeding, refreshing, and growing your starter. Although the terms are often used interchangeably, it is worth understanding the nuances.

FEEDING

Feeding the starter means you are feeding the wild yeast within the starter mixture by adding fresh flour and water. The wild yeast feeds on the natural sugars present in the flour.

REFRESHING

If you are not baking on a regular basis, it is still important to refresh your starter at least once a week. This way you are ensuring that the starter remains healthy, strong, and active, even when you are not baking. If you have neglected the starter for a while, no need to panic. You can return it to its usual vigour in a few consecutive feedings. Whatever extra starter you have (a.k.a. sourdough discard), can be used for sourdough crackers, breadsticks, pancakes, crumpets, brownies, and other delicious baked goods.

GROWING

Depending on the amount of starter you keep, you may have to grow your starter at times. You always have to anticipate how much starter is required by the recipe or for the number of loaves you plan to bake. If you have too little starter, you will need to grow it systematically. This means you will start doubling or tripling the size of the feedings according to the amount of starter you have available. Always remember to make a little extra starter or keep a small amount of backup starter in case of emergency. You don't want to get into the situation where you have used all your starter in a recipe and have nothing left to feed and grow for future bakes.

MIXING AN AUTOLYSE

Some recipes will also call for an autolyse, a mixture of flour and *all or some* of the water listed in the recipe. The yeast and salt are not added to the dough at this point. The idea is that you are assisting the gluten development without the yeast activating the fermentation process. This dough mixture is then allowed to rest for about thirty minutes, or up to several hours or overnight. This step ensures that the flour is properly hydrated and the best possible dough structure and gluten development can be obtained. The yeast (whether instant or in the form of an active sourdough culture) and the salt are added (one by one) with the help of the small amount of water that was set aside at the start of the process.

The problem with this technique is that if your mixing is inconsistent (which may be the case when mixing by hand), there is a risk of the yeast and salt not being distributed equally throughout the dough so that the final loaf has bits of yeast or salty patches. To avoid this, you can add the salt in the first step—flour, salt, and water—or simply take extra care to ensure that the dough is sufficiently mixed.

The autolyse technique is commonly used by professional bakers, but novice bakers may want to stick to straight dough breads until they are more comfortable with the basic bread-baking steps and have started to develop a better feel for and understanding of the dough, as well as the different mixing and folding techniques.

Mise en place

Mise en place is a French culinary term that means having all your ingredients neatly and conveniently placed on your work surface. It is a useful step to include in your baking (or cooking) process, as you will have everything on hand and won't have to fumble around your kitchen looking for ingredients in a mild panic. In addition to having your ingredients measured out and ready for baking, I would recommend that you also have all the baking tools you will be using close by. Trust me, you don't want to start looking for the dough scraper when your hands are already covered in dough and you are not sure exactly which drawer you left it in. Proper planning is essential and will ultimately help you achieve better results. On that note, when preparing your mise en place, you are going to weigh every ingredient as per the quantities in the given recipe. By weighing each ingredient (including the water) your quantities are going to be more accurate and you will consequently produce better and more consistent breads.

Mixing

This step requires you to mix some or all of the ingredients together according to the recipe you are using. Although you could opt to mix the dough in your stand mixer, I prefer to do this by hand, especially if it is a small batch of dough. This way you will start to develop a feel for the dough and will, over time, become attuned to what it needs (such as more or less mixing, more or less water, and so on). During the mixing stage, you will bring the ingredients together in a specific sequence. Whether you mix or knead the dough will depend on its hydration percentage: a lower hydration (less water and firmer dough) will require kneading, whereas a higher hydration (more water and wetter dough) will require mixing and folding. It is useful to work wet doughs using what is called "stretch and fold" (explained on page 40) every twenty minutes for the first hour and then to allow the dough longer intervals before the next stretch and fold (for example, every hour instead of every twenty minutes). During the mixing stage, you will notice rudimentary strings or strands within the dough. This is the beginning of the gluten formation.

Bulk fermentation (and stretch and fold)

Bulk fermentation takes place once all ingredients and starter doughs (if using) have been mixed together and the gluten has started to develop. This process usually takes place at room temperature, though some recipes may call for a cold bulk ferment (in the fridge), which slows down the fermentation process significantly (and also changes the flavour profile of the final loaf). Note, however, that you do not have to perform a stretch and fold on an hourly basis if the dough is bulk fermenting in the fridge. During bulk fermentation, the dough is generally left to ferment for four to six hours at room temperature (and longer if retarded in the fridge). The bulk fermentation time will also vary depending on the season, with warm weather leading to faster yeast activity and a shorter fermentation time and cold weather slowing down the yeast activity and calling for a longer fermentation time. The hydration percentage of the dough will also have an impact on the bulk fermentation time, with higher-hydration doughs fermenting faster than lower-hydration doughs.

Stretching and folding the dough every hour assists in the strengthening of the gluten network and will ensure that you obtain the best possible volume in your final loaf. Just as we have to exercise to strengthen our muscles, so too must the gluten strands be exercised and strengthened.

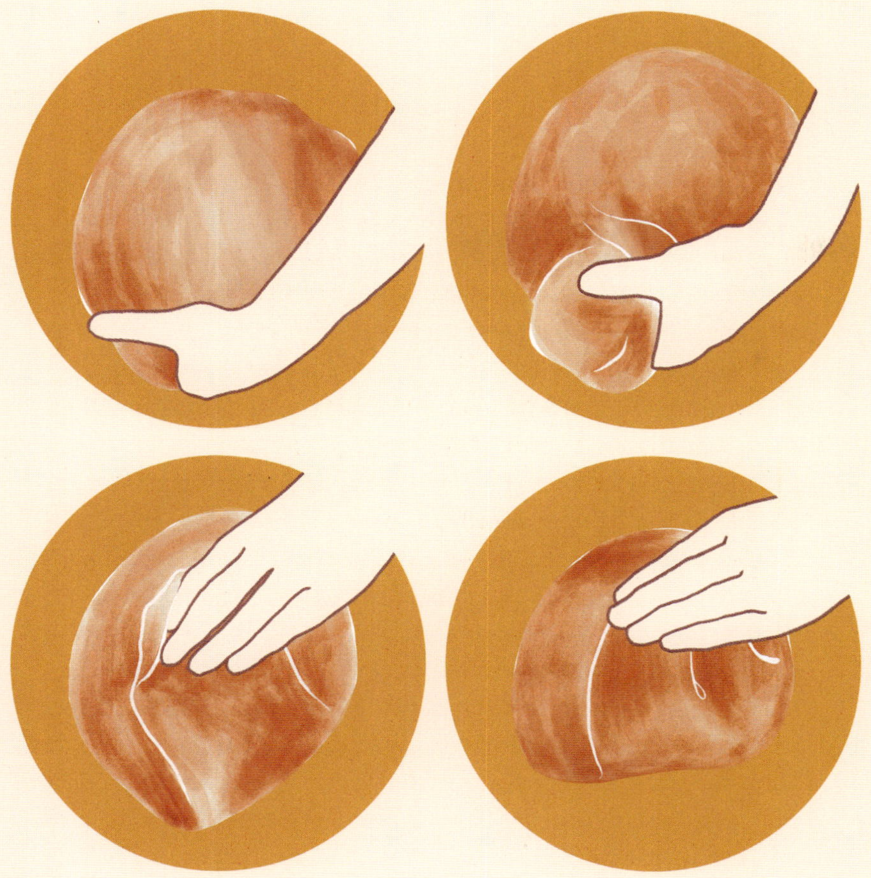

Stretching and folding is done by gently pulling the dough from the side of the bowl upward and toward the centre of the bowl. Rotate the bowl as you continue to stretch and fold toward the centre. This is done in short intervals over a period of a few hours. It is especially useful to use the stretch-and-fold technique when you have mixed the dough by hand instead of in a stand mixer. The dough will also develop its own strength during the fermentation period. As such, doughs left to ferment in the fridge for an extended period of time will still develop sufficient strength (with the exception of overly hydrated doughs and doughs mixed with low protein flours).

A well-developed gluten structure will provide the dough with enough strength to rise up and retain its shape instead of pancaking outward into a flat loaf. Flavour development also occurs during the bulk fermentation stage. When a dough undergoes a monitored fermentation period, the baker is able to manipulate these flavours. A shorter fermentation period will result in milder flavours in the final loaves, whereas a longer and/or colder fermentation will achieve stronger and slightly more acidic flavours. By playing with the fermentation *time* and *temperature*, you can manipulate and control the flavours in the final loaf. A dough that has been given a longer fermentation time will produce a crust with robust colour and wonderful depth of flavour.

Dividing, pre-shaping, and shaping

Once bulk fermentation comes to an end, it is time to divide and pre-shape your dough. Depending on the size of your dough (and number of loaves you will be baking), this may be a short or rather lengthy process. Each piece of dough is weighed and pre-shaped into a loose round, or boule. Pre-shaping assists in training the dough and gluten strands to take a specific form/shape. By pre-shaping the dough, you achieve a better structure and good volume in the final loaf. Although pre-shaping is not always necessary, this step is especially useful if you are working with a higher-hydration (wetter) dough that needs additional strength. Pre-shaping also enables an easier and more efficient final shaping process. About twenty to thirty minutes after pre-shaping, the dough can undergo final shaping, a tighter, more vigorous and deliberate shaping of the dough. The most common final shapes are the boule (round), bâtard (oval), baguette (French loaf), and small rolls or buns. When shaping loaves such as baguettes, bâtards, and sandwich breads, fold the dough in on itself as though folding a letter, before creating and sealing the seam. Alternatively, the dough can be rolled up into a tight scroll before sealing the seam. You will then place the shaped dough seam side up in a prepared bread basket (banneton) or couche (proofing cloth). The breads will proof upside down and will then be baked seam side down. Sandwich loaves and loaves that are proofed directly on a baking sheet will proof seam side down.

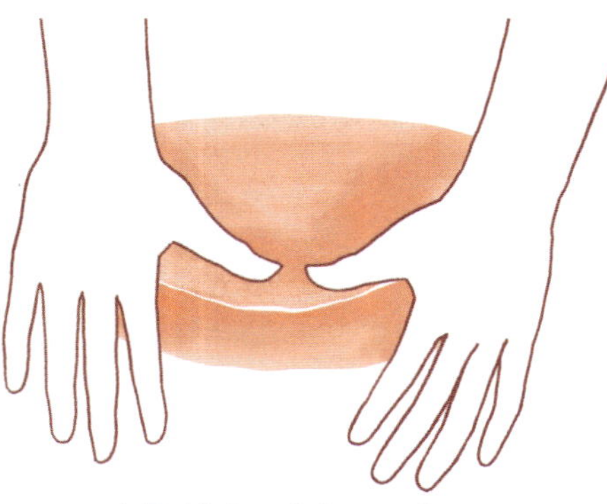

1. Fold dough inwards.

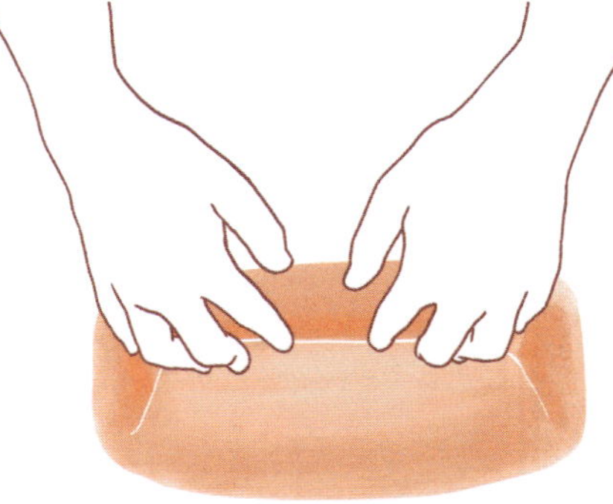

2. Fold inwards from the opposite side.

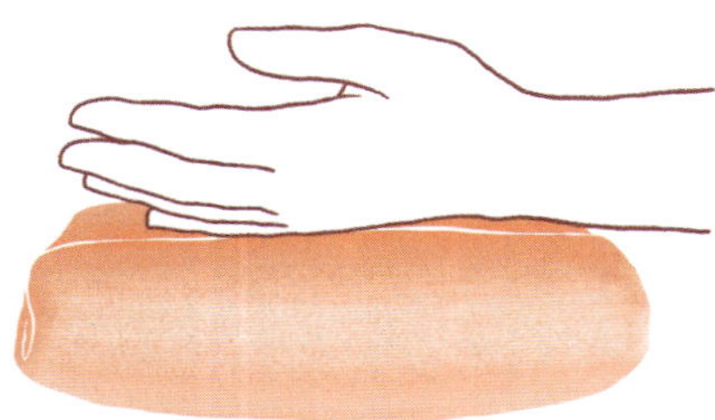

3. Create and seal the seam.

4. Shaped bâtard/loaf.

Dividing

Sealing the Seam

POSSIBLE SHAPES:

boule

bâtard

flat bread
(eg. focaccia)

miche

baguette

bread stick or thin baguette

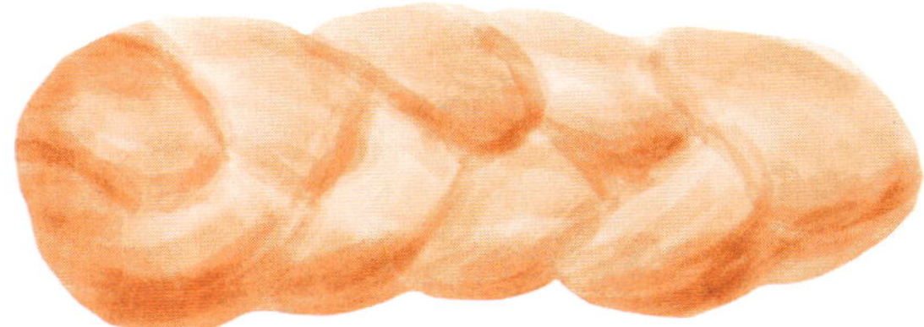

braid or plait

shaping a boule (round)
shaping a bâtard (oval/baguette)

7 Final fermentation or final proof

Once shaped, the dough will be placed in a couche (proofing cloth), banneton (bread basket), loaf pan, or simply on a baking sheet lined with parchment paper, for a final rise. The final proof is one last, short rise at room temperature or a long, slow final rise in the fridge. Here you are allowing the dough to almost double in size before baking it. Do not rush this stage, as you will be sacrificing a lovely, soft crumb and may end up with a stodgy, heavy loaf instead.

Be sure to monitor the dough so it does not over-proof. For loaves fermented at room temperature, the finger prod test is useful. Once the dough has risen for the length of time required by the recipe, gently but firmly press your finger against it. Be sure not to poke a hole into the dough; just make a visible indentation. Remove your finger and observe. If the dough springs back to its former shape and the indentation disappears, the dough needs a little longer to rise before being baked. If, however, the dough slowly makes its way to its former shape but you can still see where your finger left a mark, the dough is ready for the oven.

A final rise in the fridge will add even more flavour and character to your baked loaves. If you do this, the shaped loaves should be baked within twenty-four to forty-eight hours of being placed in the fridge.

Scoring

Before placing the shaped and proofed dough into the oven to bake, you may want to score it. The purpose of scoring is twofold.

The first reason is practical: the carefully placed cuts will guide and enable steam to rise up and out of the dough. If the steam is unable to escape, it will find weak spots in the dough and cause it to explode in various directions, leaving you with an odd looking, misshapen loaf.

The second reason for scoring is purely aesthetic: you can apply the classic cuts that will give your loaves their traditional finish or choose a unique and creative design to sign off the bake. To neatly and successfully score the dough, a baker's lame or other very sharp blade will be required (see page 15). Note that a cold final proof will make the scoring process a little easier, as the dough will have firmed up slightly.

POSSIBLE SCORING DESIGNS:

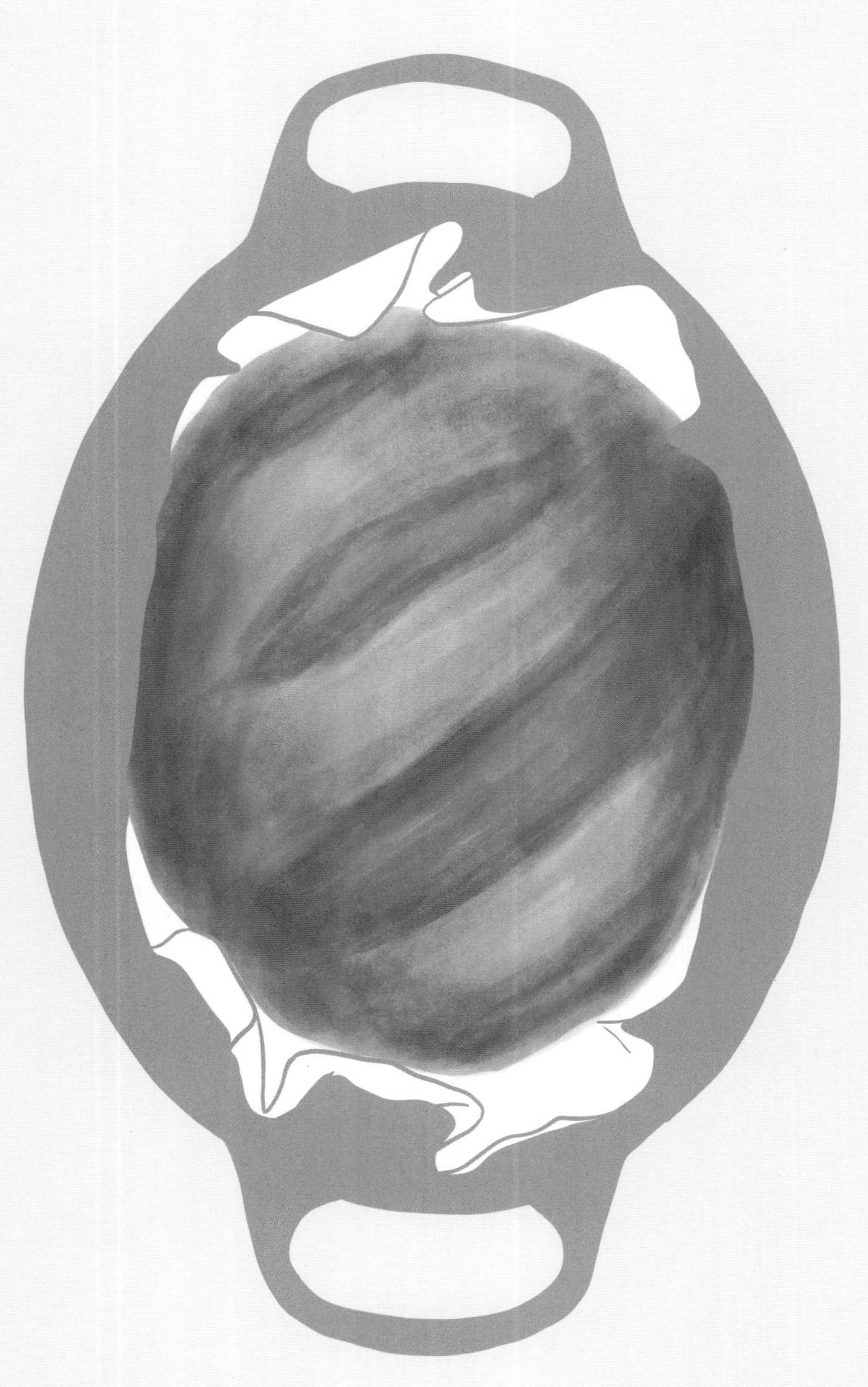

Baking with steam

You have dedicated a lot of time and done everything in your power to create the best possible environment for your dough to rise and develop. The same care is required when the dough is finally ready to face the heat of the oven. For the dough to rise to its full potential and achieve optimum "oven spring," some recipes require a good amount of steam.

Steam ensures that the outer layer (or skin) of the dough does not dry out and form a crust too quickly. Note that steam is not necessary when baking sandwich loaves and enriched breads which are baked at lower temperatures. By slowing down the crust formation, the dough is given the chance to rise (expand) one last time before turning into a loaf of bread. Without the presence of steam (especially when baking at higher temperatures), the crust will dry out and harden before the dough has risen to its optimum volume. As the loaf bakes, steam builds up inside it, causing it to rise. When the rising dough is trapped by the hardening crust, it usually results in a loaf that is flatter than expected and rather dense and stodgy. Sometimes the dough is forced to exit through weak spots (or shaping flaws), leaving the baker with a rather sad, lopsided looking loaf of bread.

To create sufficient steam to ensure a good oven spring, you have several options:

DUTCH OVEN

By using a Dutch oven or any other oven-safe vessel with a lid, you do not have to worry about creating steam at all. The environment provided by the closed pot creates a build-up of steam that is sufficient for the dough to rise optimally. As a general rule, the lid of the pot will remain on for the first twenty to thirty minutes and will then be removed, the oven temperature reduced, and the loaf given a further fifteen to twenty minutes to gain sufficient colour and caramelization of the crust. Avid home cooks will be familiar with heavy cast iron vessels (with or without enamel coating), but any oven-safe pot with a lid (including a simple enamel roaster) will easily do the job. Pullman pans function in much the same way and make it very easy to produce uniform sandwich breads. (NOTE: If you wish to avoid dark or hard crusts, you may choose to leave the lid on for longer.)

DEEP ROASTING PAN

Some bakers like to place a heavy stainless steel or cast iron roasting pan at the base of the oven. This method of steam creation requires the pan to heat up while the oven is preheating. Ice cubes or boiling water are then added to the tray to create a good amount of steam.

WATER IN A SPRAY BOTTLE

A simple plastic spray bottle (often used for plants) can be used to manually spray moisture into the oven during the bake. It is prudent to spray the sides of the oven and to avoid spraying directly on the heating element. Although this is a relatively easy way to create moisture in the oven, it has two downsides: spraying every few minutes can become a little labour intensive, and every time the oven door is opened, some of the heat will be lost.

There are, of course, many other ways of creating steam within the domestic oven and an inventive baker may like to research these. Some modern domestic ovens even come with a built-in steam function, in which case none of the above will be necessary.

OVEN TEMPERATURE

Make sure you preheat the oven as per the instructions in your chosen recipe. However, use your discretion and adjust the oven temperature as necessary. Every oven is different and no one benefits from a burned or underbaked loaf. If you use your oven regularly, you will know whether it tends to bake hotter or cooler than expected. Adjust your baking time and temperature accordingly. A baked loaf will sound hollow when knocked on the underside. When in doubt, allow the loaf to bake a little longer. If the crust is darkening too quickly, you can drop the oven temperature or loosely place a sheet of tinfoil over the top of the loaf. Most breads will be baked on the middle rack, with the exception of pizza, which requires a quick and very hot bake and therefore does better on the bottom rack (close to the element).

Babette's
Bread

10 Cooling and eating, storing and freezing

Everyone loves hot bread straight from the oven, but slicing into your fresh bread prematurely will do your loaf a disservice. The steam inside the bread won't be able to escape properly and you will be left with a stodgy loaf. The solution? Make a small bread roll along with your main loaf. Once baked, enjoy the small roll with a large dollop of butter while the large loaf cools off.

Once sufficiently cooled, the loaf can be stored in a bread bin, brown paper bag, or linen food bag. Crusty artisan loaves (especially those containing pre-ferments or sourdough) can be stored cut-side down on the breadboard. Enriched breads (eg. challahs and babkas, which are enriched with eggs, fats, dairy, and/or sugar) will last longer when tightly wrapped in cling film or a plastic freezer bag.

To freeze bread, wrap it up tightly in cling film to avoid freezer burn. To prepare frozen bread for eating, defrost at room temperature and pop it in the oven for five minutes at 356°F to restore the crust to its original crunchy glory.

Lastly, there is no reason to waste bread—especially not homemade bread. A stale, hard, dry bit of bread can easily be transformed into French toast, gourmet bread crumbs, garlic croutons, and so much more.

TRUTH BE TOLD . . .

Let me tell you a secret. You only really need a handful of staple recipes to create a great variety of delicious breads. A good lean dough (containing only flour, water, salt, and yeast) is the most versatile and useful of all doughs. With it, you can make almost any type of bread imaginable—flat breads, rolls, pizza, bagels, pretzels, vetkoek, artisan loaves, breadsticks, the list goes on. Similarly, a good, enriched dough can be used for sandwich loaves, doughnuts, cinnamon buns, beaver tails, and so much more!

But if this is true, why bother with the rest of the recipes in this book? That, dear friend, is where the magic of bread baking comes into play. The basic recipe can be likened to the ABCs, the foundation of bread baking, if you will, the root from which all other bread recipes and techniques stem. Enrichments, pre-ferments, sourdough—these are all subtle variations, the grammar, punctuation, and accent of your bread.

For example, take a basic recipe and change the amount of water in the dough, and you have created an entirely new type of bread. Or swap the water for milk and perhaps add a little butter or sugar and watch how the dough transforms yet again. Subtle changes to a basic dough will yield vastly different results in the final loaves. The recipes in this book have been carefully selected to showcase just how similar and closely connected most bread recipes really are. These recipes, whether baked in order or chosen at random, will help you become more fluent in the language of bread.

FIRST STEPS . . .

Bread baking should be fun. The process can be as simple or complicated as you choose to make it. Each person's bread needs and expectations will be different. Perhaps you would like to make a healthier version of your favourite sandwich loaf or you aim to impress your dinner guests with a rustic sourdough. Whatever your reason for baking, the basic steps remain the same. Once you have familiarized yourself with the essentials, you will easily progress to more advanced bread-baking techniques. Do not be intimidated. Trust the learning process and, above all, have fun!

Old-Fashioned Cottage Loaf with Spelt 65
The Government Loaf (Soft White Sandwich Bread) 67
Brown Sandwich Bread 71
Rustic Country Loaf 73
Rustic Flatbreads 75
Simple Milk Loaf 77

Straight Dough Breads (Direct Method)

The simplest yeasted breads involve a *straight dough* or *direct method* of mixing and baking. These breads are straightforward, making them the perfect starting point for beginner bakers. There are no starters, pre-ferments, or elaborate steps involved in the preparation of the dough. Instead, all ingredients are mixed together in a single go and the dough is baked later the same day (no lengthy delays or overnight rests). This technique offers the home baker an efficient and convenient way of producing fresh bread in a relatively short time. As an added bonus, these doughs can be easily adapted to produce a wide variety of breads.

Because this method of baking requires a comparatively short fermentation (rising) time, the resulting bread is quite mild in flavour and not as complex in character as loaves that have undergone a long, slow fermentation. This by no means renders them inferior. On the contrary, straight dough loaves are tasty and unassuming. They do not pretend to be anything they are not. Achievable, versatile, and pleasing, the straight dough loaf will introduce you to the magic of bread baking and give you the confidence to start baking on a regular basis.

NOTE: Although many straight dough recipes allow for the dough to be shaped after a single hour of rising, I urge you to allow for a minimum rising time of two hours prior to shaping. The additional rising time will result in a loaf with an overall better texture and structure.

In this chapter, you will find five basic straight dough recipes. They are great as traditional sandwich breads (baked in loaf pans), free-form loaves (baked on baking sheets), or even simple bread rolls. Beginner bakers will easily follow the baking steps and learn the process of bread baking. Intermediate and advanced bakers will find the recipes uncomplicated and may consider them a useful addition to their collection of everyday breads.

Once you have baked these loaves a couple of times, the basic workings of the dough will make sense to you and you will be ready to start adjusting the recipes by adding other ingredients, such as fruits, nuts, seeds, olives, or herbs. Alternatively, you may choose to move on to pre-fermented breads.

Old-Fashioned Cottage Loaf with Spelt

This loaf pays homage to the first loaf I ever baked, the loaf that made me fall in love with bread baking and left me hungry for more. This version calls for spelt flour, though you can easily substitute wholemeal or brown (wheat) flour. The English cottage loaf is known for its distinct shape: a small, round loaf sitting on top of a larger round loaf. Slightly lopsided, decidedly quirky, and jam-packed full of character, it pairs well with cheese and makes an equally fabulous peanut butter and syrup (or jam!) sandwich.

MAKES 1 LOAF

- 415 g / 3 ⅓ cups spelt or whole-wheat flour [83%]
- 85 g / ⅔ cup white bread or all-purpose flour [17%]
- 12 g / 2 ½ tsp salt [2.4%]
- 7 g / 2 ¼ tsp instant yeast [1.4%]
- 280–285 g / 1 ⅛ cups water (lukewarm) [56–57%]
- 45 g / ¼ cup good-quality honey [9%]
- 40 g / 3 Tbsp butter (melted) [8%]

Combine all the dry ingredients in a large bowl and mix briefly. Pour the lukewarm water, honey, and melted butter (slightly cooled) over the flour mixture. Mix the wet and dry ingredients until no dry flour is visible. The dough will feel soft and sticky but not overly wet.

Lightly dust your work surface with flour and knead the dough until it is smooth (5–10 minutes). Shape the dough into a ball, place it back in the bowl, cover it, and allow to rise for 1–2 hours, until it has doubled in size.

Line a baking sheet with parchment paper.

Lightly flour your work surface and tip the dough out. Using a sharp knife or dough cutter, cut off 290 g of dough (approximately ⅓ of the dough). To shape the cottage loaf, first shape the larger piece of dough into a firm ball and place it on the prepared baking sheet. Shape the smaller piece of dough into a round. Lightly press down on both rounds to flatten them slightly. Carefully place the smaller round on top of the large round. Use your index finger or thumb to press a hole down the middle of the stacked pieces of dough—all the way down to the baking sheet. Cover the dough with a moist kitchen towel and allow it to rise in a warm place for 60–80 minutes.

Preheat the oven to 375°F.

Bake for 40–45 minutes, until golden brown. Remove the loaf from the oven and knock its bottom to check for doneness. It should sound hollow. Allow it to cool before slicing.

NOTE: If you prefer uniform slices, you may choose to bake this loaf in a bread pan, though you will lose the old-fashioned charm of the classic shape.

Government Loaf (Soft White Sandwich Bread)

This is the loaf of my childhood, colloquially referred to as the Government Loaf. Growing up in South Africa, I distinctly remember this white sandwich bread being sold at every corner store. You could smell it baking from afar, its sweetness permeating the air and causing your mouth to water. It can be devoured in mere seconds, topped with butter, biltong (cured meat) powder, or golden syrup. It's the loaf that makes a Bunny Chow a Bunny Chow (see note). Soft and pillowy, it melts in your mouth.

MAKES 1 LARGE LOAF (OR 2 SMALL LOAVES)

- 500 g / 4 cups white bread or all-purpose flour [100%]
- 20 g / 1 ½ Tbsp sugar [4%]
- 7 g / 1 heaped tsp fine sea salt [1.4%]
- 6 g / 1 heaped tsp instant yeast [1.2%]
- 30 g / 2 ¼ Tbsp sunflower oil [6%]
- 270–290 g / 1 ⅛–1 ¼ cups water (lukewarm) [54–58%]
- Butter (for brushing the bread tin and finished loaf)

Combine all the dry ingredients in a large bowl and mix well. Add the wet ingredients and work them into a dough by stirring and massaging the ingredients together until no dry flour is visible. The dough should be firm but soft (not dry or hard). Knead the dough briefly until smooth then return it to the mixing bowl. Cover it and allow it to rise for 1 hour.

Keeping the dough inside the bowl, gently fold it in on itself or knead again briefly. Allow the dough to rise for a further hour.

Grease two 8 × 4-inch loaf pan pans with butter. (Two small 8 ½-inch Pullman pans or a large Pullman pan will work well too.)

Place the dough back on your work surface and divide into two equal pieces (if making two small loaves). Using a rolling pin, roll the dough out into a rectangle, with one side as long as the loaf pan you will be using. Roll the dough up into a long and tight cylinder (similar to rolling up the dough for cinnamon buns) and seal the seam.

Place the dough(s) seam-side down in the greased pan(s). Leave it to proof for 60–80 minutes. **NOTE:** if using loaf pans without lids, lay a sheet of cling film or a plastic freezer bag loosely over the shaped dough for the duration of the final rise and remove the plastic before baking.

Preheat the oven to 380°F.

Bake for 45–50 minutes, until golden brown. If the loaf is browning too quickly, carefully lay a sheet of tinfoil over the top of the loaf. If using a Pullman pan, remove the lid after 30 minutes and continue baking for an additional 15–20 minutes until golden brown.

Remove the loaf from the oven and brush it with melted butter (optional). Allow the bread to cool on a wire rack.

A Bunny Chow is hollowed-out sandwich bread stuffed with a spicy curry (most often mutton curry). It originated amongst the Indian South Africans of Durban.

Brown Sandwich Bread

Let's face it, no one can resist a good white loaf. But adding a little extra fibre into the mix every once in a while can only help your gut and ease your conscience. This simple brown bread recipe has a lot going for it. At 50 percent whole-grain flour, it is wholesome and nutritious. It is also wonderfully versatile and can easily be turned into sandwich breads, rolls, or even flat breads.

MAKES 1 LARGE LOAF (OR 2 SMALL LOAVES)

250 g / 2 cups white bread flour [50%]
250 g / 2 cups whole-wheat flour [50%]
7 g / 1 heaped tsp fine sea salt [1.4%]
30 g / 2 ¼ Tbsp sunflower oil or butter (melted) [6%]
6 g / 1 heaped tsp instant yeast [1.2%]
20 g / 1 ½ Tbsp sugar [4%]
315 g / 1 ⅓ cups water (lukewarm) [63%]

Prepare the dough and bake as per the instructions for the Government Loaf (page 67).

The dough can easily be divided to make 10–12 rolls, in which case, bake for only 15–18 minutes.

Allow to cool on a wire rack before slicing.

lbs
KRUPS

Rustic Country Loaf

Try your hand at this rustic loaf and add a little French country flair to your next lunch table. If you were to memorize only one bread recipe and use it for all your bread baking needs, this is the one! It is the bread I teach in all my introductory bread classes. For best results, bake this loaf in a Dutch oven.

MAKES 1 LARGE LOAF (OR 2 SMALL LOAVES)

500 g / 4 cups unbleached white bread flour* (preferably stone-ground) [100%]
10 g / 1 ¾ tsp fine sea salt [2%]
5 g / 1 tsp instant yeast [1%]
350–375 g / 1 ½–1 ⅝ cups water (lukewarm, volume depending on humidity and/or preference) [70–75%]
20 g / 1 ½ Tbsp extra virgin olive oil (optional) [4%]

*SUBSTITUTION: *In place of the unbleached white bread flour, you can use a combination of white and whole-grain flour, adding up to 500 g (4 cups) in total.*

Place all the dry ingredients in a large bowl. Add the water and olive oil (if using) and fold together until a basic dough has formed and no dry flour is visible. The dough will feel quite wet and soft but should hold together. Cover and allow it to rise for 3 hours, giving the dough a stretch and fold (see page 40) every hour.

After the third hour of bulk fermentation, the dough should be light, airy, and well risen (with good gluten structure). It is now ready for shaping. Dust a bread basket with flour. Lightly dust a counter with flour and gently tip out the dough. Shape it into a tight round or oval and dust with a little flour. Place the shaped dough into the prepared basket, seam side up. Loosely cover with a clean dish towel or a sheet of cling film and allow to rise for 30–45 minutes.

Preheat the oven to 450°F. (If using a cast iron Dutch oven, place the vessel in the oven while it is preheating and be careful not to burn yourself when transferring the dough to the pot or covering with the lid. Enamel Dutch ovens do not have to be preheated.)

Transfer the dough to a sheet of parchment paper. Gently lift the paper and dough into the Dutch oven. Score the top of the dough with a baker's lame or very sharp blade.

Bake in the preheated oven, covered, for 25 minutes. Remove the lid, drop the temperature to 430°F, and bake for a further 20–25 minutes, or until golden and crusty. The loaf should sound hollow when tapped/knocked underneath. (When in doubt, bake for 5–10 minutes longer.)

This loaf pairs well with butter, cheese, and strawberry jam.

Rustic Flatbreads

Using any of the straight dough bread recipes, you can produce wonderfully versatile flatbreads. Top them with olive oil and herbs or brush them with egg wash and sprinkle with sesame seeds. These breads make a beautiful addition to any meal and are particularly well suited to sharing and tearing.

MAKES 1 LARGE FLATBREAD (OR 3 SMALL FLATBREADS)

1 batch Rustic Country Loaf dough (page 73) or Government Loaf dough (page 67)

Olive oil and za'atar topping

25–30 g extra virgin olive oil

Za'atar* (for sprinkling on top)

Sesame seed topping

1 egg

2 Tbsp Greek yogurt, milk, or water

Black and white sesame seeds

**Za'atar is a Middle Eastern spice mix consisting of sumac, thyme, sesame seeds, salt, and sometimes other spices.*

Prepare one batch of either the Rustic Country dough or the Government Loaf dough.

Line a baking sheet with parchment paper.

When the dough has fermented as per the instructions in your chosen recipe, tip it out onto a well-floured countertop. Lightly dust the surface of the dough with flour (just enough to create a thin layer of flour and enable handling the dough without it sticking to your fingers). Divide the dough into 2–3 pieces. Gently stretch each piece into the desired flatbread size and place on the prepared baking sheet(s).

Cover with a damp kitchen towel and allow to rise for 30–40 minutes, until puffy.

Preheat the oven to 420°F.

For the za'atar topping, drizzle the dough with the olive oil, then top with the za'atar. For the sesame seed topping, whisk the egg together with the yogurt, milk, or water, brush it on the dough, then top with the sesame seeds. Next, dimple the dough with your fingertips. To do this, use one or both hands to gently (but firmly) press (dimple) a series of indentations across the surface of the dough (about ⅔ into the dough but not poking holes all the way through).

A large flatbread will bake for about 25–30 minutes, while the three smaller ones will require 15–20 minutes.

Serve warm with your favourite meze or tapas.

Simple Milk Loaf

Milk lends a wonderful richness to bread doughs and yields loaves with soft, fluffy interiors. At 88 percent water, milk can easily be substituted for water in most bread recipes. Case in point, this milk loaf is based on the white sandwich bread recipe on page 67 but calls for lukewarm milk instead of water and butter instead of oil. This dough is ideal for braiding (plaiting) but can also be turned into pull-apart loaves, soft flatbreads, or fancy rolls.

MAKES 1 LARGE LOAF (OR 2 SMALL LOAVES)

500 g / 4 cups white bread or all-purpose flour [100%]
20 g / 1 ½ Tbsp sugar [4%]
7 g /1 heaped tsp fine sea salt [1.4%]
30 g / 2 ¼ Tbsp butter (melted) [6%]
6 g / 1 heaped tsp instant yeast [1.2%]
270–290 g / 1 ⅛–1 ¼ cups milk (warm) [54–58%]
Butter (for brushing the baked loaf)

Weigh out all the ingredients.

Combine the dry ingredients in a large bowl. Add the lukewarm milk and melted butter to the flour mixture. Mix together to form a firm but soft dough.

Lightly flour a countertop and knead the dough for 5–10 minutes. Return the dough to the bowl, cover, and set aside to rise for 1 hour.

Working inside the bowl, knead the dough again briefly. Cover and allow it to rise for an additional hour.

Line a half baking sheet with parchment paper.

Divide the dough into 6 pieces for 2 loaves, and 4 pieces for a Pullman pan. Using a rolling pin, roll each piece into an oval approximately 6–8 inches long. Roll the dough up tightly and place 3 pieces into each pan or 4 pieces into the Pullman pan. Cover the dough loosely with clingfilm and allow to rise for 60–80 minutes.

Preheat the oven to 420°F.

Bake the risen loaves uncovered for 30–35 minutes. They should be beautifully golden and sound hollow when tapped underneath. Place on a cooling rack and brush with butter (optional).

LET'S STEP UP OUR BREAD GAME!

Now that you have mastered straight dough loaves, you are ready to start playing with pre-ferments. If you were wondering how to add flavour and character to your bread without having to understand or own a sourdough starter, the pre-ferment is sure to excite you. Do not be put off by having to prepare the pre-ferment in advance—the five minutes it takes on Day 1 will save you several hours the next day, as the bulk fermentation time will be reduced significantly. As pre-ferments need to be mixed several hours (or days) in advance, it is essential to plan ahead. The best way to do this is to decide when you want the bread to be ready and then to work backwards to determine when to prepare the pre-ferment and when to add it to the final dough. (Don't get me wrong, I am all for spontaneous baking, just not when poor planning means having to bake at midnight!)

Rustic Country Bread with Pâte Fermentée 87

Kalamata Olive Breadsticks 89

Baguette with Poolish 91

Epi Baguette (Wheat Stalk Baguette or Ear of Wheat Bread) 97

Ciabatta with Biga 101

Pre-Fermented Breads

Pre-ferments are a great addition to every baker's box of tricks. When used correctly, they have the power to coax incredible flavour, strength, and character out of the dough in a relatively short time. As an added bonus, pre-ferments act as natural preservatives, allowing the bread to stay fresh much longer than straight dough breads.

Making a pre-ferment involves mixing a small portion of flour with water and a little bit of yeast or sourdough culture and allowing the mixture to develop for a few hours or overnight. Thus it is "previously" fermented. This fermented mixture is then added to a new dough, which is again left to ferment, before being shaped and baked. In order to control the fermentation (so the pre-ferment does not over-ferment, which will result in bread that is flat, dense, and acidic) be sure to use only enough yeast to inoculate the dough and get the fermentation process started.

The three most common pre-ferments are pâte fermentée, poolish, and biga (though some enriched doughs like the Montreal Bagels on page 205 call for a sponge).

Of the three, the simplest pre-ferment is the pâte fermentée, also called "old dough." As the name suggests, it is essentially a piece of bread dough that, instead of making its way into the oven, was left to ferment. The pâte fermentée contains flour, water, salt, and yeast, and is thus considered a complete dough. To bake with it, simply reserve a small amount of bread dough from one batch of dough for use in a subsequent batch. A pre-ferment can be kept in the fridge for up to three days before the yeast will run out of food and energy.

Poolish and biga, on the other hand, are prepared specifically as pre-ferments. Neither of the two contain salt, so you need to slightly increase the amount of salt in the final dough to achieve a balanced flavour.

Where a poolish is a very wet (high hydration) pre-ferment, a biga is much firmer and contains less water. It is possible to use any pre-ferment (whether liquid or stiff) in doughs of high or low hydration provided the amount of water in the final dough is adjusted to accommodate the hydration percentage of the chosen starter. If the recipe is not adjusted to compensate for the lack or surplus of water in the pre-ferment, the final dough may not reach the desired consistency (may be too wet or too firm).

Professional bakers employ varying amounts of pre-ferments to produce very specific types of breads. Even a small amount of pre-ferment can significantly improve the structure, taste, and colour of the final bread. These qualities are carefully developed by means of controlled fermentation of both the pre-ferment and the final dough. Using a large amount of pre-ferment in a recipe, although possible, should be done with care, as the rate (speed) of fermentation can become difficult for a beginner baker to control.

For this reason, the amount of pre-ferment called for in each of the following recipes is relatively small. Each recipe is designed to showcase the workings and application of a particular type of pre-ferment. As such, the quantity of water, flour, and salt varies according to the type of pre-ferment being used. These recipes are intended as examples and guidelines, not hard and fast rules.

Baker's percentages

You'll notice that the ingredients lists in my recipes include percentages. Beginner bakers may choose to stick to the measurements, whereas more advanced bakers will find the percentages useful—especially when adapting a recipe to their specific needs. Learning about baker's percentages is useful because it's how professional bakers think about their recipes. Baker's percentages represent each ingredient as a percentage of the flour content, which is always considered 100 percent. To determine the percentage of a particular ingredient, the ratio of that ingredient in relation to the amount of flour must be determined. Don't panic, I promise it is not difficult! Here's how it works.

As I said, the flour in any given recipe is always read as 100 percent. Each of the other ingredients fall within a specific range, as follows:

To calculate the percentage of each ingredient in a recipe, divide the weight of the ingredient by the weight of the flour. Here's an example:

1,000 g flour
= 100% (always)

800 g water
= 800 divided by 1,000 = 0.8 x 100 = 80% hydration

20 g salt
= 20 divided by 1,000 = 0.02 x 100 = 2%

4 g instant yeast
= 4 divided by 1,000 = 0.004 x 100 = 0.4%

200 g pâte fermentée (pre-ferment)
= 200 divided by 1,000 = 0.2 x 100 = 20%

NOTE: The pre-ferments in this chapter are prepared with instant yeast, making this technique accessible to bakers who are not yet familiar with sourdough. They can be substituted with the same amount of liquid or stiff sourdough starter (in accordance with the hydration percentage of the pre-ferment called for in the recipe). If using sourdough, omit the instant yeast and allow for a bulk fermentation period of a minimum of 4 hours. Proceed as per your usual sourdough method.

Pre-ferments offer a fantastic way of adding character and flavour to your bakes. They bridge the worlds between straight dough breads and sourdough breads—not quite as simple and plain as the former and definitely not as involved as the latter. In other words, the best of both worlds.

Rustic Country Bread with Pâte Fermentée

You may recognize this country bread from the previous chapter. However, this version offers even better structure and character. In addition to the qualities provided by the old dough, the small amount of rye adds lovely colour and depth of flavour. The rye can be substituted for whole-wheat flour or all white bread flour, if you prefer. This recipe beautifully showcases how even a small amount of pre-ferment can drastically improve a simple straight dough recipe.

NOTE: If you haven't reserved a 100 g piece of dough from your last bake, you'll have to make up a small batch of pâte fermentée the day before you want to bake (see Day 1 below). If you have pâte fermentée, jump ahead to Day 2.

MAKES 1 LARGE LOAF (OR 2 SMALL LOAVES)

Day 1 (for the pâte fermentée)

62 g / ½ cup flour
38 g / ⅛ cup water
Pinch instant yeast
Pinch salt

Combine all ingredients in a medium bowl. Work the mixture into a dough and allow it to rise at room temperature for 1 hour before transferring it to the fridge overnight (or for up to 3 days). The mixture may also be left to ferment at room temperature overnight.

Day 2

100 g / ½ cup pâte fermentée (old dough) [20%]
450 g / 3 ½ cups white bread flour (preferably unbleached) [90%]
50 g / ½ cup rye flour* [10%]
11 g / 1 ¾ tsp fine sea salt [2.2%]
4 g / 1 tsp instant yeast [0.8%]
350–375 g / 1 ½–1 ⅝ cups water (lukewarm, volume depending on humidity and/or preference) [70–75%]
20 g / 1 ½ Tbsp extra virgin olive oil (optional) [4%]

**In place of the rye flour, a total of 500 g (4 cups) of white bread flour may be used.*

Remove the pre-ferment from the fridge and set aside. It's best if it reaches room temperature before being added to the main dough.

Combine all the dry ingredients in a large bowl. Add the water, olive oil (if using), and the pâte fermentée. Mix well until no dry flour is visible. Cover and set aside. (You will notice that the addition of the pre-ferment quickly adds strength to the dough, creating elasticity and accelerating the gluten development.)

Return to the dough after 1 hour and perform a few stretches and folds (see page 40). Cover the dough and set aside for an additional hour.

Dust a proofing basket and countertop with flour.

Gently tip the dough out onto the floured work surface. Shape into a large oval or round. Place the shaped dough in the proofing basket and allow to rise for 30–45 minutes.

Preheat the oven to 450°F.

Transfer the dough onto a sheet of parchment paper (just big enough to lift the dough into the Dutch oven). Carefully lift the paper and dough into a Dutch oven. Using a baker's lame or sharp knife, score the surface of the dough (see page 50). Bake covered in the preheated oven. After 25–30 minutes, remove the lid of the Dutch oven. Continue baking for an additional 20–25 minutes, until golden brown and crusty. The loaf should sound hollow when knocked underneath.

Allow to cool on a rack before serving.

Kalamata Olive Breadsticks

Olives are my Achilles' heel. I can eat them by the jar, if not by the bucketload! These soft bread-sticks are jam-packed full of Kalamata olives, my absolute favourite, though you could swap them out for green or black olives or whatever you happen to have on hand. Be sure to remove the pits before adding the olives to the dough—and perhaps add a splash of olive brine for extra flavour! Enjoy as is or as part of a delicious meze platter, charcuterie board, or selection of antipasti.

MAKES 25 SOFT BREADSTICKS

1 batch of Rustic Country Bread dough, including the pâte fermentée (page 87)
200–220 g / 1 ¼–1 ½ cups Kalamata olives (pitted and roughly chopped)

After 3 hours of bulk fermentation, return the dough to the bowl and scatter the olives over the top. Gently stretch and fold the dough (see page 40) over the olives to distribute them throughout the dough. Cover and set aside for 1 additional hour.

Tip the dough out onto a countertop dusted with flour. Divide into 25 equal pieces (approximately 50 g each). Gently stretch and roll (if possible) each piece of dough into strips of about 10–12 inches.

Line 1 or more baking sheets with parchment paper.

Place the dough strips onto the baking sheets, leaving ⅜-inch gaps between each piece. Cover with clean kitchen towels and allow to rise for 20–30 minutes.

Preheat the oven to 430°F.

Bake the breadsticks for 15–18 minutes, until just starting to turn golden. The crust should be leathery and the bread-sticks should give way when pressed.

Baguette with Poolish

One of the most iconic breads of all time and the pride of France, a crusty baguette is beautiful to behold and a pleasure to consume—paired, of course, with a good cheese and a decent bottle of wine. This recipe calls for a poolish, a pre-ferment first used by Polish pastry chefs and later adopted by French bakers. Baguettes are best eaten the day they are baked, but stale loaves can be transformed into rather fabulous garlic bread (page 249).

Making a good baguette takes practice and a lot of patience. Be sure to adjust the amount of water in the recipe according to the protein content (and level of absorbency) of your flour. To be safe, start with less water and add only as much as the flour can comfortably absorb. (If the dough is too soft or weak, the final baguettes will be quite flat.)

MAKES 3 SMALL BAGUETTES (OR 6 DEMI BAGUETTES)

Day 1 (for the poolish)

75 g / ½ cup bread flour

75 g / ⅓ cup water

Pinch of instant yeast

Combine all the ingredients in a jar and mix well. Cover and allow to ferment overnight. (If the poolish won't be used for baking the next day, it can be kept in the fridge for 2–3 days.)

Day 2

150 g / ¾ cup poolish [30%]

500 g / 4 cups baguette flour or strong white bread flour (± 13% protein) [100%]

285–340 g / 1 ¼–1 ⅜ cups water [57–68%]

11 g / 2 ¼ tsp fine sea salt [2.2%]

3–4 g / 1 level tsp instant yeast [0.6–0.8%]

After the poolish has fermented overnight (or longer), observe it. The fermentation should have brought about a multitude of small bubbles across its surface and it should smell fragrant and somewhat fruity. If you give the jar a gentle shake, the mixture will respond with a pleasing little jiggle.

In a large bowl, combine the poolish with the remaining ingredients and mix for 5–10 minutes, until no dry flour is visible. Cover and set aside for 1 hour.

Return to the dough and perform a series of stretches and folds (see page 40). The dough should feel elastic and strong. Cover and set aside for an additional hour.

Tip the dough out onto a work surface lightly dusted with flour. Divide it into 3 or 6 equal pieces and loosely pre-shape them into rounds. Cover the rounds and set aside for 15–25 minutes.

Shape the baguettes (or demi baguettes) by gently pulling the dough into oval/rectangular pieces (approximately 6–6 ½ inches). Place one piece in front of you horizontally on the lightly floured countertop and fold the top half toward the centre as you would when folding a letter. Rotate the dough 180° and fold toward the centre again. Continue folding and tightening the dough until it feels firm and somewhat compact (not loose or weak). To join the two folds of dough and create a seam, gently but firmly press the base/palm of your hand down on the edge of the folds, sealing them together. Continue pressing and sealing along the length of the dough until one long seam has been formed. (You will hear little bubbles popping as the folds of dough are sealed together.)

Set out a couche (proofing cloth) or large piece of parchment paper. Turn the dough over so that the seam is facing down, under the dough. Start to roll (not drag!) the dough from the centre outwards. As you roll, the dough will become longer. Repeat with the other dough pieces.

Once you are happy with the length of your baguettes (aim for about 12–15 inches) or demi baguettes (6–8 inches), place the shaped loaves in the folds of the couche or parchment paper, folding the paper up like a drape to separate them. Cover and allow to rise for 45 minutes to 1 hour.

Preheat the oven to 470°F. This bread requires plenty of steam. (See page 53 for options to create steam.) If you are using the pan method, preheat the pan/skillet as the oven preheats.

Transfer the baguettes from the couche onto a baking sheet or carefully slide the parchment paper onto the sheet, opening/flattening the folds of paper. Score each loaf with a sharp knife or baker's lame.

Place the scored baguettes (or demi baguettes) in the preheated oven and add a good amount of ice cubes to the pan/skillet at the bottom of the oven. Close the oven door and bake with steam for 15 minutes. Carefully remove the pan/skillet of steaming water and continue baking until golden brown and crusty—approximately 10–20 minutes longer for the 3 baguettes and 5–10 minutes longer for the 6 demi baguettes.

Allow to cool on a rack before serving.

At the bakery in Maboneng, the late Mr. Washington Makoto (a wonderfully talented Zimbabwean baker) and I would shape hundreds of baguettes every week. These went out to wholesale customers in and around Johannesburg. Back at the bakery, the baguettes were cut in half and used to produce our popular Gourmet Baguette Sandwiches.

Epi Baguette (Wheat Stalk Baguette or Ear of Wheat Bread)

This unique loaf makes a beautiful addition to the communal table. It is produced in much the same way as the classic baguette but is given a whimsical twist by cutting the dough so it resembles a wheat stalk. Once baked, the wheat florets (kernels) can easily be separated into individual bread rolls—perfect for sharing!

MAKES 2 LARGE EPI BAGUETTES

1 batch Baguette with Poolish dough (page 91) or any firm bread dough that can be rolled and shaped

Divide the risen baguette dough (once bulk fermentation is complete) into 2–3 equal pieces. Follow the instructions in the Baguette with Poolish recipe (page 91) to pre-shape and shape the dough.

Cover and allow the baguettes to rise for 35–40 minutes.

Preheat the oven to 470°F.

Generously dust a sheet of parchment paper with flour and place the risen baguettes on it. Using a pair of clean kitchen scissors, cut into the dough at 45° angles. Start cutting at the base of the baguette and continue moving upward, making sure to only cut halfway or three quarters of the way through the dough. (Be careful not to sever the pieces entirely.) After each cut, lay the cut piece to the left and the next piece to the right, alternating as you make your way toward the top end of the baguette. (Make sure there is enough flour under the cut pieces so they do not stick to your fingers or the paper.) You can make the cuts as small or large as you like, depending on how many pieces you want.

Bake in the preheated oven for 25–30 minutes, until golden and crispy, or a little longer, depending on your oven and personal crust preference.

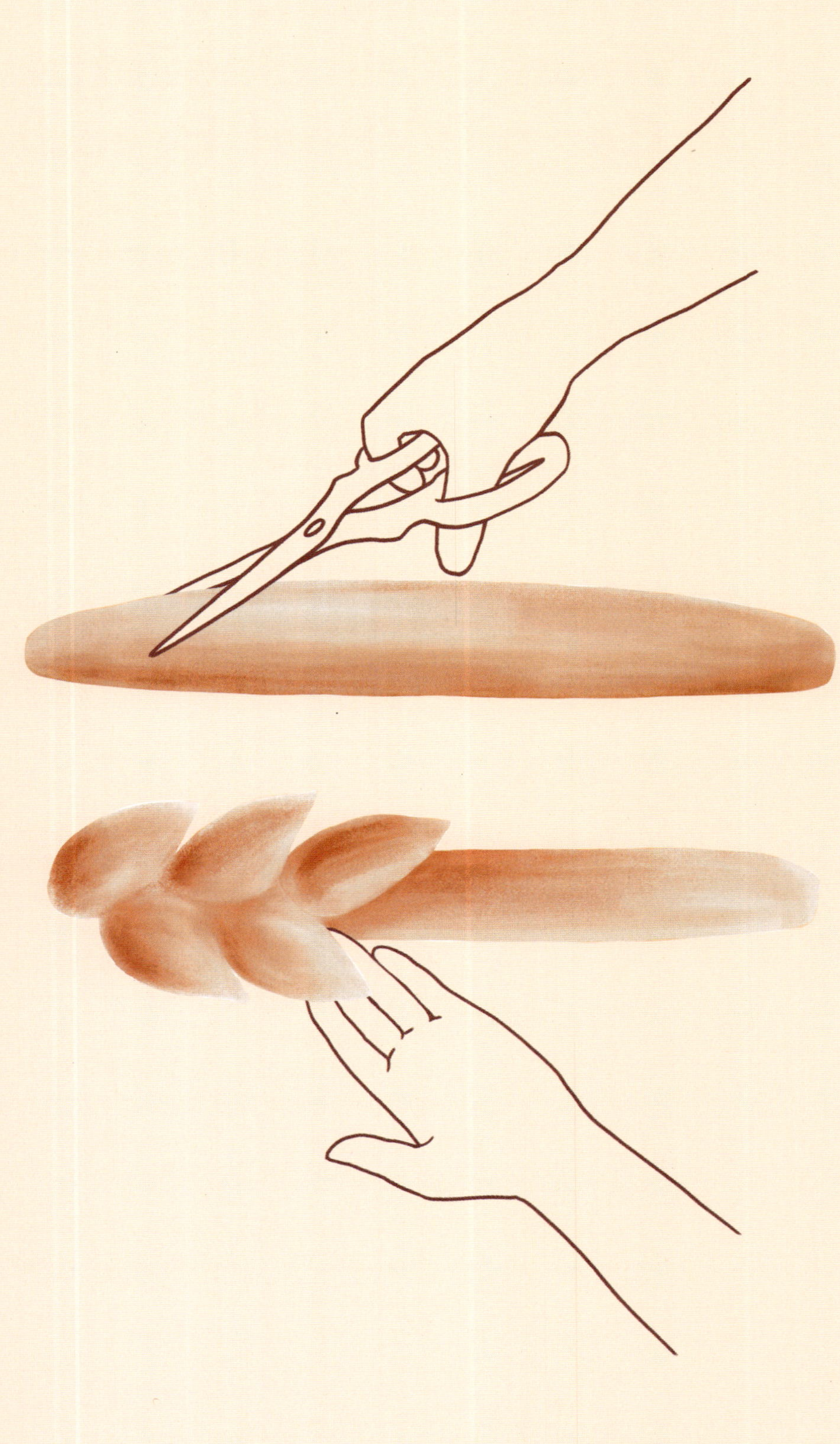

Ciabatta with Biga

This classic slipper-shaped bread is the Italian answer to the French baguette. Countless versions and interpretations can be found all over Italy. The ciabatta is the perfect vessel for mopping up golden olive oil, meaty gravies, and delicate sauces. With its subtly nutty flavour (thanks to the biga), it doesn't need any additions—but adding olives to the dough once in a while makes for a delectable twist.

NOTE: The pre-ferment in this recipe is a stiff-dough (firm) biga. Though in Italy the word *biga* refers to both liquid and firm pre-ferments, if using a liquid pre-ferment (poolish), be sure to adjust (reduce) the hydration in the final recipe. Although it is possible to mix ciabatta dough by hand, you may find it easier to use a stand mixer to work the rather wet and soft dough.

MAKES 4 MEDIUM CIABATTAS (OR 6–8 PANINIS / BREAD ROLLS)

Day 1 (for the biga)

- 135 g / 1 cup bread flour
- 75 g / ⅓ cup water (just enough water to mix into a firm dough)
- Pinch of instant yeast

Combine the ingredients in a small bowl. Knead briefly until no dry flour is visible. Shape into a ball, cover, and allow to ferment at room temperature overnight (or up to 3 days in the fridge).

Day 2

- 150–200 g / ¾–1 cup biga (pre-ferment) [30–40%]
- 500 g / 4 cups strong bread flour (high protein)
- 12 g / 2 tsp salt [2.4%]
- 380–420 g / 1 ⅝–1 ¾ cups water [76–84%]
- 20 g / 1 ½ Tbsp olive oil (optional) [4%]
- 200–220 g pitted Kalamata or green olives (optional) [± 45%]

Uncover the biga and observe it. The overnight fermentation should have created a somewhat risen and puffy ball of dough. The dough may be starting to collapse in on itself (deflating), but it should not have receded completely. You will also notice a few small holes (signs of fermentation) dotted across the surface of the dough. The biga will smell fragrant, wholesome, and nutty.

Combine all the dry ingredients in a large bowl or the bowl of a stand mixer. Add the water and olive oil (if using) and mix until all the dry flour is incorporated. The dough will be rather wet and sticky. Cover and allow the dough to rest for 15 minutes.

Cut the biga into smaller pieces and add to the mixing bowl. Work the dough until the pre-ferment is fully incorporated and there are no lumps. The biga will quickly add strength and structure to the dough, making it much easier to handle. If you used a stand mixer, transfer the dough to a clean mixing bowl. Cover the mixing bowl and set aside for 1 hour. Return to the dough and perform a few stretches and folds (see page 40). Cover and set aside for an additional 1–2 hours.

Tip the dough out onto a well-floured countertop and generously dust its surface with flour. Using a dough cutter (or your hands) gently push against the sides of the dough, giving it a somewhat rectangular shape. If the dough is too sticky, dust with a little extra flour. Cut the dough into 4 equal rectangular pieces (or 6–8 paninis) with your dough cutter. Dust the newly cut edges with a little flour to prevent them from sticking.

Line a baking sheet with a large piece of parchment paper and dust it with flour. Gently transfer the first piece of dough to the parchment and fold the paper to create a pleat (to keep the adjacent piece from sticking). Repeat with the remaining pieces of dough, creating pleats between them. Gently pull the paper pleats together so the pieces of dough are resting against each other but remain separated by the folds. Cover with a kitchen towel and allow to rise for 50–60 minutes.

Preheat the oven to 500°F. This bread requires steam. (See page 53 for options to create steam.) If you are using the pan method, preheat the pan/skillet as the oven preheats and have a bowl of ice on hand to add to the pan once the ciabattas have been placed in the oven.

Uncover the dough and pull the edges of the parchment paper to flatten the pleats.

Bake in the preheated oven for 5 minutes, then drop the temperature to 450°F and bake for an additional 15–20 minutes, until the loaves are golden and crusty. Transfer the ciabattas to a wire rack and listen for the crackling of the crust as it cools.

Any high-hydration dough, whether straight dough, made with pre-ferment, sourdough, or cold fermented, can be used to produce ciabatta-style breads. Although the resulting breads will look similar, there will be subtle differences of flavour and texture unique to the chosen method of fermentation.

There is nothing romantic about getting up in the middle of the night or the early hours of the morning—especially in winter! It goes against every fibre of one's being and the natural human inclination to seek comfort and warmth under the covers just that little while longer. It is 2:00 AM and my alarm clock has just gone off. Shivering, I get dressed and make my way next door, to the small home bakery my parents helped set up for me. (My sisters will confirm with glee that I was a most unlikely candidate to embrace these hours—until I discovered bread baking.)

I check on Maggie (the sourdough levain), wrapped in her heavy duvet, and am relieved to find the beanbag still radiating some heat. The starter is not ready to be used yet, needing another hour or so. Perhaps two. I switch on one of the ovens to start warming up the room, then remove a large, rectangular container of cold-fermented dough from the fridge. After fourteen hours of retardation, it will now rest at room temperature for two to three hours before it gets portioned and shaped into baguettes.

Next, I lift the lid of the poolish (pre-ferment) and give the container a little shake. The silky, bubbly mixture jiggles in response, giving off a yeasty fragrance and a promise of good bread. My eyes glance over the day's orders: thirty country loaves, forty sourdoughs, and fifty baguettes. Not too bad for a little home bakery! I start weighing the dry ingredients, placing the flour into large plastic buckets, and the salt and yeast into their own separate containers.

With everything prepared, before I start the great task of hand mixing (as I do not yet own a dough mixer), I have a few precious minutes to myself. Wrapped in a large shawl, I sit down on the red brick stairs outside the bakery to enjoy a large mug of black coffee and a handful of buttermilk rusks. I soak up the stillness. This is the magic of the wee hours, reserved for those who are up long before the crack of dawn, meticulously and consistently honing their crafts, while the rest of the world is still sleeping. When everything is dark, quiet, and peaceful. These are the reflective hours. Creative hours. Contemplative hours. Alone with one's thoughts and senses. No company but the excited chitter of birds welcoming the new day and the first rays of sunlight gently breaking the dark sky.

Cold-Fermented Focaccia 109
Fougasse 111
Pizza Dough 114
Koulouria (Greek Sesame Bread Rings) 117
Pot Bread (Potbrood) 119

Cold-Fermented Breads

The fridge is your friend. This may at first feel counterintuitive, but befriending your fridge will improve your overall bread baking and will definitely come in handy when you are faced with a difficult dough or impending baking disaster. On hot summer days, when the yeast is particularly active, you may want to pop the dough in the fridge to slow down the fermentation and yeast activity. The cooler environment will prevent the dough from over-fermenting, weakening, and losing its shape and structure. As an added bonus, the cold fermentation will produce excellent flavour in your final breads.

Placing your dough in the fridge will be useful in the following situations:

1. When you want to slow down the rate of bulk fermentation on a particularly hot day.
2. When you are making a cold-fermented bread—where the dough is mixed using ice-cold water and immediately placed in the fridge overnight for a cold bulk ferment. There are two options for working with this type of dough the next day: (1) Scale and shape the cold dough and allow for a long final rise at room temperature. Note that when the dough is particularly wet, it will be easier to shape when cold. (2) Remove the dough from the fridge and allow it to come to room temperature before shaping and allowing for a shorter final rise.
3. When the dough has bulk fermented at room temperature, the shaped loaves can have a long, slow cold final fermentation period in the fridge. This will make for easier scoring/slicing of the surface of the dough before baking and provide a little more flexibility in terms of when you bake the loaf (for example, thirty minutes before your lunch guests arrive). If the loaves were retarded in the fridge overnight and you are using a Dutch oven, they can be baked straight from the fridge and do not need to come to room temperature prior to baking.
4. When you simply need to ensure that the dough doesn't over-ferment or do anything unexpected while you pop out of the house for a few hours. Placing the dough in the fridge for a couple of hours will slow the fermentation and ensure that you have a healthy and happy dough to work with when you get home. You can remove the dough from the fridge and continue as normal, or leave it in the fridge and shape it the next day.

If you have paged through older recipe books or spoken to your grandmother about bread baking, you may be under the impression that bread dough always requires warmth and yeast will only activate and work in ideal conditions and temperatures. However, the advent of instant yeast has revolutionized the world of bread baking. This yeast no longer needs to be "activated" with sugar and lukewarm water (although the latter always helps on chilly days). All ingredients can now be added together all at once, instead of in multiple cumbersome (and sometimes confusing) steps.

The idea of allowing your bread dough to rise in the fridge instead of somewhere warm and cozy may at first be a little daunting, but this technique (or a version of it) will soon prove useful. If the convenience of not having to stay awake until the early hours of the morning to bake your bread because you got your timing wrong and started too late in the day doesn't convince you, the flavour and character of the final loaf will most certainly win your heart. This method of fermentation is ideal for rustic focaccias and pizzas—although a long, cold fermentation will coax flavour out of any bread dough.

Cold-Fermented Focaccia

This easy overnight focaccia is perfect for simple sandwiches or for mopping up delicious gravies and hearty soups. It is mixed with ice-cold water and will spend most of its time in the fridge. Although the dough requires very little hands-on time, it produces pretty impressive results. And if the idea of cold fermentation is not enough to pique your interest, you are bound to enjoy dimpling a beautifully bubbly focaccia dough!

Keep your toppings simple and let the bread do the talking.

NOTE: I recommend doubling the recipe for an extra-spectacular loaf, but remember to use a larger sheet pan!

MAKES 1 MEDIUM FOCACCIA

- 500 g / 4 cups white bread or all-purpose flour
- 5 g / 1 tsp instant yeast [1%]
- 10 g / 2 tsp fine sea salt [2%]
- 350–400 g / 1 ½–1 ¾ cups water (ice cold, volume depending on the type of flour used) [70–80%]

Toppings

- 42 g olive oil
- 2–3 cloves of garlic (finely chopped)
- 10 g rosemary
- 5 g coarse salt or salt flakes

Day 1: Combine all dry ingredients in a large bowl. Add the water and mix until no dry flour is visible. Cover and place in the fridge overnight. (NOTE: the dough will rise despite the cold conditions so be sure to choose a large enough container).

Day 2: Remove the dough from the fridge and allow it to rest at room temperature for 2–3 hours. The dough will wake up and should become rather bubbly.

Line a ¼ or ½ size baking sheet with parchment paper.

Drizzle a little olive oil onto the baking sheet and use a pastry brush (or your hands) to lightly coat the parchment with the oil. Tip the dough out onto the oiled paper. Gently spread and stretch the dough across the entire surface of the tray. Allow the dough to rise for 1 hour.

Preheat the oven to 430°F.

Drizzle olive oil over the dough and scatter with garlic (if using), rosemary, and coarse/Maldon salt (or use your own choice of toppings).

Thoroughly dimple the surface of the dough with your fingertips to create the characteristic focaccia look. The dimples will reduce the amount of air in the dough slightly and prevent the dough from rising or puffing up too quickly in the oven. To do this, spread your fingers apart (pretend that you are going to play the piano or type on a keyboard) and gently but firmly press your fingertips into the dough. Repeat at intervals across the surface of the dough. The idea is not to flatten the dough completely but to "dock" the dough with your fingertips to prevent it from ballooning and completely changing its shape. Bake in the preheated oven for 25–30 minutes, until golden brown.

This loaf is great for sharing and tearing. Serve it hot from the oven and watch it disappear in no time!

FUN FACT: The cold slows down the yeast activity resulting in a bread with more subtle and nuanced flavours, which would not have developed during a short fermentation at room temperature.

Fougasse

Both the Italian focaccia and the French fougasse are derived from an ancient Roman bread called *panis focacius*, from the Latin word *focus* meaning hearth or fireplace. Panis focacius was originally a kind of test bread, baked amongst the embers of the hearth to determine the temperature and readiness of wood-fired ovens. Keep it plain, or top it with a little olive oil, herbs, and salt and pepper. In the South of France, common additions are black olives, garlic, cheese, and anchovies. Slash the dough with a knife or metal bench scraper and stretch it into decorative leafy shapes prior to baking.

MAKES 1 LARGE OR 2 SMALL FOUGASSES

1 batch Cold-Fermented Focaccia dough (page 109)

Additions and toppings

2 large heads of garlic or 200 g Kalamata or black olives (pitted)
42 g olive oil
10 g fresh thyme
5 g salt flakes

Day 1: Prepare a batch of Cold-Fermented Focaccia dough and let it rise in the fridge overnight.

Day 2: Remove the dough from the fridge and allow it to stand at room temperature for 2 hours.

While the dough is resting, roast the garlic (if using).

Preheat the oven to 350°F.

Slice off the top part of the head of garlic to expose the individual cloves. Carefully remove a few layers of the papery outer skin. Place each head of garlic on a piece of tinfoil (approximately 2 × 2 inches), drizzle with olive oil, and sprinkle with a pinch of salt. Wrap the garlic up in the foil and twist or crimp to close it off at the top. Place each wrapped head of garlic in a ramekin or other oven-safe vessel and roast in the preheated oven for 45–50 minutes. Allow to cool.

Unwrap the garlic and gently remove (squeeze) the buttery cloves from the outer husk.

Tip the dough out onto a countertop lightly dusted with flour, but do not add more flour to the surface of the dough. Gently stretch the dough out as much as possible—without tearing it. Distribute the roasted garlic (or olives, anchovies, cheese, etc.) and fresh thyme equally across the surface of the dough, then fold the dough up and over itself until you have a little parcel. Thus, the additions will be ensconced within the layers of the dough. This technique is referred to as lamination. Lightly press down on the dough to encourage the layers to stick together. Cover and allow to rest for 45–60 minutes.

Preheat the oven to 450°F. This bread requires steam. (See page 53 for options to create steam.) If you are using the pan method, preheat the pan/skillet as the oven preheats and have a bowl of ice on hand.

Line a baking sheet with parchment paper and lightly dust with flour.

If you are making the large fougasse, leave the dough whole. If making the 2 smaller ones, use a metal bench scraper or sharp knife to divide it. You can eyeball the portions or use a kitchen scale if you want the pieces to be of uniform weight and size. Gently lift each piece of dough, stretch it to the desired size and thickness (remember the dough will still rise when baking in the oven), and transfer it to the prepared baking sheet. Turn the tray so the dough lies horizontally. Using the metal bench scraper, make 3–5 diagonal incisions into the dough, taking care to leave ¾–1 ¼ inches uncut on either side and not sever the pieces entirely. Angle the cuts so the lines spread outward to resemble a hand-held fan. Gently stretch the dough to open the cuts and give the dough a leafy appearance. Repeat if you have a second piece of dough.

Brush the dough with olive oil and sprinkle with the salt flakes. Bake in the preheated oven with steam for 20–25 minutes, until golden brown and crusty. Allow to cool before serving.

Pizza Dough

This simple Italian flat bread is beloved around the world. Topped with beautiful fresh produce, bursting with flavour, and smothered in cheese—what's not to love? And when it comes to variations, the options are endless! From thick or thin bases, tomato or bechamel sauces, traditional toppings (rather than the somewhat controversial pineapple or banana), folded, wood-fired, deep-fried—there is a pizza for everyone!

A pizza dough containing a pre-ferment (page 91–92), a sourdough starter (page 35–37), or that has had a good long rest in the fridge will always yield a pizza with better flavour and texture.

NOTE: If you do want the benefits of a long, cold rise, start this 2–3 days ahead so you can let the dough rise in the fridge.

MAKES 4 (12-INCH) PIZZA BASES

500 g / 4 cups bread flour
11 g / 1 ¾ tsp fine sea salt [2.2%]
4 g / 1 tsp instant yeast [0.8%]
310–350 g / 1 ¼–1 ½ cups water [62–70%]
30 g / 2.2 Tbsp olive oil [6%]
15 g / 3 tsp full-fat milk (optional) [3%]

Combine all the dry ingredients in a large bowl. Add 310 g (1 ¼ cups) of water along with the olive oil and milk, and knead until smooth. Add more water sparingly and only if the dough is too dry (unless you are specifically intending to work with a higher hydration pizza dough*). Continue mixing until the dough comes together. It should be soft but not overly wet. Cover and allow to rise for 1 hour.

Return to the mixing bowl and give the dough a few stretches and folds (see page 40). Allow the dough to rise with hourly stretches and folds for an additional 2–3 hours. At this point you can place the dough in the fridge for 2–3 days to develop extra flavour, or simply proceed with dividing and shaping.

If refrigerating, remove the dough from the fridge and allow it to stand at room temperature for 1–2 hours.

Divide the dough into 4 equal pieces. Pre-shape it into loose rounds and cover for 15–20 minutes.

Preheat the oven to 480°F. Prepare pizza pans by lightly dusting with flour or line baking sheets with parchment paper.

Shape each round into a disc by stretching and pulling by hand (recommended) or roll out as thinly as possible (or as per your preferred thickness). This will require a bit of patience. If the dough isn't playing along, allow it to rest for approximately 5 minutes (to relax the gluten) and then continue stretching/rolling it out. Place the dough discs on the prepared pizza pans or baking sheets. Using a spatula or the back of a spoon, spread a thin layer of sauce over each base and top with your choice of toppings.

Bake on the lowest rack of the preheated oven for 10–15 minutes, until the crust is well baked and no longer doughy. Top with fresh basil, arugula, or slices of avocado and enjoy! (As every oven is different, it is prudent to check the pizza bases about 8–10 minutes into the baking time to ensure that they are not burning.)

**A higher hydration dough will yield more than four pizza bases—but will also be trickier to handle.*

HOTEL HELLENIC
PRETORIA

Koulouria (Greek Sesame Bread Rings)

These large, ring-shaped sesame breads are a hugely popular breakfast or anytime snack food in Greece. In Turkey, the same bread is known as *simit* and in different parts of the Mediterranean and Middle East, it goes by yet other names. Before being coated in sesame seeds and baked, the rings are usually dipped in plain water or water mixed with honey, petimezi (Greek grape-must syrup/molasses), or rosewater and sugar. Although koulouria are usually kept plain, they can also be stuffed with black olives, feta cheese, or various other fillings.

MAKES 8–10 SESAME RINGS

500 g / 4 cups bread flour
5 g / 1 tsp instant yeast [1%]
7 g / 1 ¼ tsp fine sea salt [1.4%]
260–280 g / 1–1 ¼ cup cold water [52–56%]
30 g / ¼ cup extra virgin olive oil [6%]
45 g / 2 Tbsp honey [9%]

Toppings

125 g petimezi / pekmezi (or honey) diluted in 65 g of water
120–150 g sesame seeds

Combine the dry ingredients in a large bowl. Add the water, olive oil, and honey and slowly start stirring the ingredients together. Work into a basic dough by kneading, folding, and massaging the ingredients together. The dough should be firm but not dry. Cover and allow to rest for 1 hour. Return to the dough and give it a few stretches and folds (see page 40). Cover and place in the fridge overnight. (If you intend to make the koulouria the same day, allow for a minimum of 2–3 hours of bulk fermentation.)

Remove the dough from the fridge and allow it to sit at room temperature for 1–2 hours.

Gently tip the dough out onto a lightly floured work surface. Divide into 8–10 equal pieces. Roll each piece into a long rope about as thick as your index finger. Join (squeeze) the ends together and set aside until all the rings have been formed.

Prepare a large baking sheet (or a few smaller baking sheets) by lining with parchment paper.

Dilute the petimezi, pekmezi, or honey in 65 g of water—a wide and shallow bowl works best. (Alternatively, use plain water.) One by one, dip the rings of dough into the liquid. Roll them in sesame seeds. Place the rings well apart on the prepared baking sheet(s). Allow the dough to rise for 30 minutes.

Preheat the oven to 390°F.

Bake the sesame rings for 15–20 minutes, until golden brown. Transfer to a cooling rack and be sure to eat at least one koulouri (one koulouri, many koulouria) while still hot from the oven and pretend that you are on holiday in Greece. *Kalí* órexi*!*

Pot Bread (Potbrood)

Potbrood can be baked right in amongst the coals—a novel project for the outdoor enthusiast—though it can just as easily be baked in a domestic oven. This dough can be prepared in advance and kept chilled, ready to impress your fellow campers or barbeque guests. Be sure to use a heavy cast iron pot if you do decide to brave the coals, or risk serving charred bread for dinner. Serve as a side to grilled meat and salad or for breakfast with butter, cheese, and apricot jam.

NOTE: This is a two-day bread, so start it the day before you want to bake it.

MAKES 1 LARGE POT BREAD

- 1 batch of dough from the Government Loaf (page 67), Rustic Country Bread (page 87), or Simple Milk Loaf recipe (page 77).
- Butter for greasing the Dutch oven

Day 1

Prepare your desired dough. Allow the dough to rise at room temperature for 1 hour then place it in the fridge/cooler overnight.

Day 2

Baking in hot coals

Prepare a wood or charcoal fire, then remove the dough from the fridge or cooler and allow it to rest at room temperature until the flames start to die down.

Grease a large cast iron Dutch oven (minimum 7 quart / 6.6 litres) with butter. Shape the dough into a ball or oval. Place the dough in the greased Dutch oven, cover, and allow it to rise for 45–60 minutes, until well risen.

Once only hot coals remain, shift the coals away from the centre of the fire, creating a ring.

Position the Dutch oven inside the ring of coals, packing the cinders snugly against the pot. A few hot coals can also be placed directly on top of the cast iron lid. Bake for 45–60 minutes, until golden brown and cooked through. (NOTE: the pot is surrounded by coals and does not sit directly on top of the coals. Thus it is sitting on the residual heat from where the fire was burning.)

Baking in a domestic oven

Grease a cast iron Dutch oven with butter or oil. Remove the dough from the fridge or cooler and shape it into a ball. Place the ball of dough in the greased Dutch oven, cover, and allow it to rise for 45–60 minutes, until well risen and at least doubled in size.

Preheat the oven to 390°F.

Bake for 30 minutes, with the lid on. Remove the lid and bake for an additional 10–15 minutes until golden brown. Allow the bread to cool for a few minutes before turning it out onto a cooling rack. If you prefer a softer crust, wrap the hot loaf in a large kitchen towel while it cools.

It is hard to imagine a time before the comfort and conveniences of the modern home kitchen. Of fridges and electrical appliances. A time when creative solutions had to be found in order to put bread (or a simple meal) on the table. The popular Afrikaans saying "n' boer maak n' plan" translates to "a farmer makes a plan." The expression acknowledges the tenacity and inventiveness required to survive hard times. It serves as an encouraging reminder that a clever solution can (and will) be found.

When the first Dutch traders arrived in the Cape and established a trading post colony, they were tasked with setting up kitchens (which they called *kombuise*, after the word for a ship's galley) in order to feed the growing number of transient peoples. To bake their bread, they used hollowed-out ant heaps or holes in the ground. Hot coals were placed inside these cavities, which were then sealed with large stones to create rudimentary but functional ovens. Naturally, the heavy-duty cast iron Dutch oven, or *potjie*, became the cooking vessel of choice and is still a common feature in many South African households today.

It is still dark when we arrive at the bakery in Maboneng—downtown Johannesburg. The Main Street lights provide just enough illumination for us to find our way into the old building (previously home to a cut glass business) and up the stairs. Within seconds, the fluorescent light flickers to life, then blasts through the magnificent cottage pane windows, illuminating the bakery like a giant lantern in the night.

Saturdays are the busiest days at the bakery. Today, my husband, Vasili, is baking with me, helping me lift and carry the large bags of unbleached stone-ground flour and the heavy tubs of dough. We have a lot to do and are a little pressed for time, with loadshedding (planned power outages) due to start in only a few hours. To a playlist of '80s and '90s rock, we set to work. We prepare a great variety of doughs: sourdough, baguette, rye, rustic country, ciabatta, rolls, and more!

I place the lid on the last batch of dough, just as Mekdes and Solomon arrive with two black coffees, Americanos brewed from Ethiopian coffee beans, specially sourced for their coffee shop. Now the dough needs time to work its magic, giving us the opportunity to catch up on admin. Vasili sends out invoices, while I double check the orders and prepare the packaging—large sheets of brown paper and labels with the Babette's Bread logo. Coffee and sesame breadsticks keep us going.

A few hours later, the dough is ready to be portioned. We shape the dough into long, thin baguettes, hefty bâtards, robust boules, and cute little rolls. As we work, the rising sun steadily makes its way from the windowsill down onto the granite counter, bathing first the dough and then our hands in the morning light. Down below, Main Street is already bustling with activity as early morning commuters make their way about town.

The baguettes are first to leave the oven. Lined up on cooling racks, they proudly show off their distinct cuts and beautiful curves. As I load the bread baskets with fresh bread, I cannot help but think of the late Mr. Washington. Washington Makoto. An exceptionally talented and most personable Zimbabwean baker, with a work ethic second to none. He tragically passed away in 2020, leaving behind his partner, Brenda, and young son, Jayden.

The last loaves of 100 percent rye come out of the oven and I breathe a sigh of relief. We made it. Still a good few minutes before the power is due to go off. All the loaves are out, in the process of cooling or being wrapped. We are ready to start our deliveries.

Sourdough 101 124
Beginner's Sourdough 133
Everyday Easy Eating Rye 135
The Apprentice Loaf 138
Gérard's Sourdough (Pain au Levain) 141
Greek Village Bread (Horiatiko Psomi) 143
Sourdough Sandwich Bread 147

Welcome to the Wild Yeast . . . Here There Be Micro-organisms

It might surprise you to learn that we are at all times surrounded by countless micro-organisms and cultures. More specifically, strains of wild yeast and different types of bacteria. These wild yeast spores, along with friendly bacteria known as lactobacilli are of particular importance to bakers, as they hold the key to a vast world of naturally leavened breads and other baked delights.

Both of these organisms are naturally present in our everyday environment (in the air around us, on the fruit in the fruit bowl at home, on the surface of furniture, our skin, and so on) and when they are combined within the sourdough starter mixture of flour and water, they develop a symbiotic relationship. The lactobacilli break down the complex carbohydrates (in the flour) and turn them into simple sugars for the wild yeast to feed on. During this feeding process, the yeast releases carbon dioxide, which allows the starter mixture to rise. A further by-product of the breakdown of the sugars is the production of the sour/tangy flavours that sourdough breads are known for.

The wild yeast will continue to feed on the natural sugars in the flour until they are depleted. Once the yeast has run out of food, it quite literally runs out of steam, and the starter will stop rising and slowly begin to collapse in on itself. By regularly feeding and refreshing the starter, the baker is able to maintain a healthy wild yeast culture—a culture that, with the right care, may be perpetuated indefinitely.

Sourdough 101

With a healthy, happy sourdough starter, you can produce naturally leavened breads with great flavour. Because this bread is partially pre-digested by the wild yeast and other micro-organisms, it is easier on the human stomach and much more flavourful than commercially leavened breads. The long fermentation time required by sourdough baking also naturally extends the shelf life of the bread. That is, it acts as a natural preservative.

Similar to pre-fermented breads, sourdough baking requires you to mix a small portion of dough in advance (in this case, sourdough starter), which will be left to ferment and later added to the final dough. The different hydration percentages of the pre-ferments can also be likened to the different types of starters bakers use around the world, namely stiff starters (+/- 50% hydration) and liquid starters (+/- 100% hydration), or even a starter with a hydration percentage somewhere between 50% and 100%.

However, sourdough starters are not quite as straightforward as just mixing the starter and setting it aside until needed the next day. The sourdough starter's activity needs to be monitored and timed. To properly plan the bake, you need to understand how long it takes for the starter to reach its prime level of ripeness. Although it is possible to bake with a starter that is already past its optimum level of ripeness, it may not always give rise to the perfect loaf.

To determine and understand your starter's schedule, you can place an elastic band around the jar indicating the level of the starter just after feeding it. Alternatively, you can make a mark on the jar with a white-board marker. NOTE: It is useful to pay special attention to the starter (and the dough) during seasonal changes. The fermentation time might need to be increased (or decreased) by several hours for the desired dough volume and texture to be achieved.

Next, take note of the time. By monitoring the time, you will be able to determine how long it takes for the starter to double or even triple after a feeding, before running out of steam (carbohydrates to feed on) and starting to recede/collapse again. The ripening time required by your starter will become predictable the more often you feed and monitor it. You may, for example, notice that your starter tends to double after four hours and triple after five or six hours.

Each starter is unique. Its rising/ripening time will depend on the hydration percentage of the starter, how much culture was used in the feeding process (the ratio of starter to flour to water), the type of flour used, the ambient temperature in the room or on the particular day, and the health and strength of your starter.

You can control the rising and fermentation time of a starter by adjusting the hydration percentage and/or the feeding ratio of the starter. As a general rule, a liquid starter will ferment much faster than a stiff starter. This is because a higher amount of water makes it easier for the yeast to access and feed on the natural sugars in the flour. The stiff starter, on the other hand, will require the wild yeasts to work much harder to reach and consume the natural sugars, resulting in a much slower rise. Of course, stiff starters are fed with a higher flour-to-water ratio, so there is more flour for the yeast to work through. (For example, I feed my stiff starter as follows: 50 g starter + 60 g water + 100 g flour.)

DIFFERENT APPROACHES

Before you get started on making your very own sourdough starter, please understand that there is no one way to make (and bake with) sourdough starters. In fact, the art of cultivating a yeast culture of some sort to leaven bread is prevalent in many cultures around the world. There are numerous approaches to the making, feeding, and use of these starters.

Also note that not all sourdough starter cultures are started or maintained with wheat flour. Some are derived from potatoes (South Africa), pineapples, teff flour (Ethiopia), fermented chickpeas (Greece), fermented raisins, and other types of yeast waters. Others are fed with flour, milk, and sugar. And yet other sourdough starters require the addition of a small amount of salt. Each approach differs from the next, yet people have managed to bake beautiful, nourishing bread for thousands of years.

I know a few experienced home bakers who simply mix some starter, flour, and water together, allow the mixture to rise, and then go on to bake wonderful bread. Basic bread, yes. Unpretentious bread, you bet. But wholesomely delicious and extremely satisfying, nonetheless. And if you ask them for a specific recipe or ratio, they just shrug their shoulders and smile. They learned by watching their mothers, who in turn had learned from their mothers, and so the tradition continues. In our modern world, it is easy to forget that there was a time before scales and weighing implements, a time before any means of measuring exact quantities. And yet, bread was being baked. Good bread. Nourishing bread. Life-sustaining bread.

I have also heard mention of several traditional sourdough bread recipes that call for the starter to be used once a thin layer of liquid has risen to the surface of the starter mixture. This thin layer of liquid is referred to as hooch. In modern baking, this layer means the starter is hungry and requires feeding. And yet, many traditional breads were and still are baked in this way! So remember, there is more than one way to bake sourdough bread.

Another approach used by some bakers is to feed their starters by measuring a portion of the starter and then adding half the starter's weight in flour and the other half in water. (In other words, a ratio of 1: ½: ½. See the next page for more about ratios.) This method of feeding allows for a fast, reliable rise and produces very mild-tasting (non-sour) loaves. It is not celebrated by all bakers, but then again who wrote the law on sourdough baking?

In short, there are many opinions out there. I often feel that more experienced bakers are too unforgiving of the methods used by home bakers. Bread is bread after all. And if the chosen method produces bread that is safe to eat, nourishing, and satisfying, who is anyone to judge?

CONVENTIONAL STARTER RATIOS

With more modern sourdough methods, most bakers feed their starters using a very specific ratio. The ratio refers to the amount of starter, water, and flour used in a feeding. These ratios range from 1:1:1 to 1:2:2 and up to 1:5:5 or even higher. The first number refers to the amount of starter used in the feeding and the last two numbers refer to the amounts of water and flour.

For example:

10 g starter + 10 g water + 10 g flour (1:1:1)
10 g starter + 20 g water + 20 g flour (1:2:2)

The size of the feeding ratio will directly affect how quickly or slowly the starter will rise. The smaller the ratio (1:1:1), the faster the rising time. The less starter and more food (flour) in a particular feeding (say, 1:5:5), the longer and slower the rise will be. By playing around with the ratios, bakers are able to fit their bread-baking activities into their everyday schedule.

STARTER MAINTENANCE AND BEST RESULTS

To ensure maximum starter strength and optimum wild yeast activity in their starters, professional bakers feed their starters every day, and sometimes twice daily. This is obviously not practical or sustainable for home bakers.

In my opinion, it is sufficient to refresh your starter once a week and to do at least two to three consecutive feedings leading up to a bake. This will ensure that the starter is sufficiently active and able to produce good bread. Although it is certainly possible to bake bread after a single feeding, the secret to great sourdough success is a happy and very well (and regularly) fed starter. In the end it boils down to what you are looking to achieve in your bakes. Bread baking is a rather forgiving process. It can be as simple, complicated, or time-consuming as you have patience and energy for.

If you are not baking on a regular basis, the starter will survive well in the fridge. You will want to keep it as small as possible (20–50 g or ⅛–¼ cup) but it should ideally be fed once a week. You can always grow or build your starter in the feedings leading up to your next bake. Remember, the more starter you keep, the more you will need to feed it. You may eventually end up with an insatiable starter, rather like the Audrey II in *Little Shop of Horrors*. (Besides, you can only bake and eat your way through so many sourdough discard recipes.)

For best results, use the starter when it has at least doubled (or more!) in size after being fed. This will ensure that it is strong and active enough to leaven a loaf of bread.

FACT VS. FICTION

Some bakers maintain that the older the starter is (in years), the better the performance of the starter and the quality of the bread. This is not the case. Over time, and with every feeding, the wild yeast organisms are replaced by new and different strains. As such, a one-hundred-year-old starter is not so different from the three-month-old starter you have been meticulously caring for. The natural yeasts are continuously refreshed and replaced in both the old and new starters.

Similarly, as soon as the starter moves from one baker and one kitchen to the next, it undergoes significant changes. The natural yeasts present in the new kitchen, on the new baker's hands, and in the new type of flour used for feeding the starter immediately start to change the original sourdough culture. As a result, no two cultures are the same—even if they originated from the same culture.

However, there is something endearing about owning and baking with an "older starter"—one that has been passed down from one generation to the next. The romance and nostalgia of producing bread the same way our grandparents did is understandable. You would be forgiven for believing you are baking with the very same starter your great-grandmother used. It connects us to our past, provides a sense of community, and encourages us to keep the tradition going. Sourdough cultures have a curious way of working themselves into the heart of the family and household. Most bakers name their sourdough starters and care for them like one would a favourite pet. Once a good baking rhythm is established and the starter's importance to the family is recognized, it becomes an honorary member of the family. Sometimes it even gets to tag along on holidays—or, in my case, on honeymoon!

I maintain three wheat sourdough starters: Maggie, Honey, and Tahini (see photo on page 129) and have just added a gluten-free starter named Sylwia to the collection. Maggie (ten years old at the time of writing) is my stiff-dough French levain, which I first made at the bakery in Vermont. Honey (three years old) is one of the three liquid sourdough starters I created as part of a Facebook tutorial when Covid-19 had just started; like her name suggests, the initial culture was made from a mixture of flour, water, and honey. Tahini (one year old) was created as part of a step-by-step YouTube series on making your own sourdough starter; she is maintained (fed) with a mixture of white and freshly milled dark rye or spelt flour. Sylwia is maintained with brown rice flour and may be featured in a future book.

Make Your Own Sourdough Culture

To make a standard size loaf of bread, you will require between 50 and 100 g (between a ¼ and a ½ cup) of ripe and refreshed starter.

You can make your own sourdough starter by mixing flour and water together and leaving the mixture to ferment. This mixture will require refreshing and feeding for the next 5–7 days (sometimes a little longer). For additional guidance, have a look at my step-by-step Sourdough Starter Tutorial on YouTube.

Day 1: In a glass jar, mix 50 g (¼ cup + 1 Tbsp) bread flour (preferably stone-ground and unbleached) with 50 g (⅕ cup) lukewarm water (a teaspoon of honey or rye flour is optional). Place an elastic band around the jar (or use a marker pen) to indicate the level the mixture is at in the jar. Cover loosely with the lid and set aside in a warm place for 24 hours.

Day 2: Observe the starter and check for any signs of life (bubbles). Has it risen above the elastic band or marker line at all? Add a further 50 g (¼ cup + 1 Tbsp) of flour and 50 g (⅕ cup) of water and mix well. Set aside again in a warm place for 24 hours.

Day 3: Observe the mixture and check for bubbles. Has it risen and/or collapsed? Remove half of the mixture (100 g / ⅓ cup + ½ Tbsp) from the jar. Feed the remaining 100 g with 50 g (¼ cup + 1 Tbsp) flour and 50 g (⅕ cup) water. Set aside in a warm place for 24 hours.

Days 4–7: Continue as per Day 3 and observe the development of the bubbles and yeast activity over a couple of days. It is quite common for a thin layer of liquid to appear on the surface of the culture. This is called "hooch" and is an indication that the starter is getting too hungry between feedings. Simply mix the hooch back into the mixture, discard half, and start feeding the starter every 12 hours instead of 24 hours.

Similarly, if the starter shows signs of having doubled (above the line) but subsequently collapsed again, it is clearly running out of food between feedings. From now on, you can feed the culture every 12 hours instead of every 24 hours. At this point you may also start feeding the starter according to a 1:1:1 ratio, meaning 50 g / 3 Tbsp starter + 50 g / ⅕ cup water + 50 g / ¼ cup + 1 Tbsp flour.

During these 7 days (approximately), you should try to get an understanding of the culture's unique schedule/cycle and feeding requirements. By using an elastic band or making a mark on the glass container immediately after a feeding, you will be able to determine (use a timer!) how quickly the starter doubles or triples in size after being fed. This can be anything between 2 and 8 hours after a feeding. Once the starter consistently doubles within a certain (predictable) period, you are ready to bake your first loaf of sourdough bread!

If for some reason your starter is not taking off at all and not becoming bubbly (even after a few days of regular feeding), it may be that the environment is too sterile. Avoid using harsh chemicals and/or cleaning materials in the starter's immediate environment. (Remember, we want to attract and encourage the wild yeast!)

> **"Let me see your hands," the baker said. "Good. Yes. Strong, wide hands. Working hands. Baker's hands."**

Beginner's Sourdough

Don't be intimidated by the following (long) list of instructions. Instead, view it as me holding your hand every step of the way.

But before you jump into the recipe, make sure that you have established a good relationship with your starter and have a decent understanding of its unique schedule and rhythm. (That is, how long does it take to double or triple in size after a feeding?)

Once you have baked a couple of loaves, you will realize that a recipe is merely a framework in which you will need to make some well-calculated adjustments. Under perfect conditions, a recipe can be followed to a T, but in reality every baking day introduces a unique set of variables that you as the baker will need to navigate.

MAKES 1 LARGE LOAF OR 2 SMALL LOAVES

- 500 g / 4 cups white bread or all-purpose flour [100%]
- 10 g / 1 ¾ tsp fine sea salt [2%]
- 350–375 g / 1 ½ cups water (lukewarm) [70–75%]
- 100 g / ½ cup liquid sourdough starter (at prime level of ripeness) [20%]

Combine the flour and salt in a large bowl. Add the desired amount of water and the ripe starter to the bowl and mix until no dry, floury bits are visible. Cover the dough and set aside in a warm place for 20 minutes.

Return to the dough and perform a few stretches and folds (see page 40). Note that the dough should be lukewarm to the touch. If it feels cool or cold, move it to a warmer location after the stretch and fold. You can repeat the stretch and fold every hour for 4–5 hours. After about 5 hours, the dough will be ready to shape. It should be soft, airy, and a little puffy. If not, allow for a further 1–2 hours of fermentation. (Remember that the dough will behave differently depending on the season, the weather conditions, the ambient temperature, etc. on the given day. So you as the baker will need to observe and adjust your timings accordingly.)

Flour 1 or 2 bannetons or proofing baskets, depending on whether you are making 1 large loaf or 2 small loaves.

Shape the dough into 1 or 2 tight rounds or ovals and transfer to the banneton(s). You can allow the dough to rise at room temperature for another 2–3 hours, but I recommend placing it in the fridge for a minimum of 12 hours.

Once your dough has proofed (at room temperature or in the fridge), you are ready to bake. Preheat your oven to 450°F. Also preheat your cast iron Dutch oven.

Dust the shaped dough with a little flour to prevent it from sticking to the base of the Dutch oven. Gently tip the dough into the Dutch oven. Score/cut the surface of the dough with a baker's lame or very sharp blade. Bake in the preheated oven, covered, for 25–30 minutes.

Remove the lid and bake for a further 20–25 minutes or until the crust is beautifully golden and caramelized. Knock the base of the baked loaf and listen for a hollow sound. When in doubt, bake for an additional 5–10 minutes.

As the loaf cools, listen for the crackling sound of the crust. Bakers refer to this crackle as the "singing of the loaves."

Everyday Easy Eating Rye

When I was three years old, we lived in Maastricht in the Netherlands for three months. Apart from the fantastic playgrounds, decadent hagelslag (Dutch chocolate sprinkles), sticky stroop-wafels (Dutch waffle cookies), and the statue of the musketeer D'Artagnan (made famous by Alexandre Dumas's stories), Maastricht also introduced little Babette to RYE bread. One fine afternoon, my mother placed a large pre-sliced loaf of rye on the lunch table. She buttered two slices and handed us one each. Cautiously, we took our first bites. I will never forget the floral flavour that hit my young taste buds!

MAKES 1 LARGE LOAF OR TWO SMALL LOAVES

Day 1: Starter

- 140 g / 1 ⅓ cups dark rye flour
- 110 g / ½ cup water
- 6 g / ½ Tbsp ripe sourdough starter

At 7:00 PM, combine all the starter ingredients, cover and leave in a cool place for 24 hours (not in the fridge).

Day 2–3: Dough

- 500 g / 4 cups white bread or all-purpose flour [100%]
- 12 g / 2 ½ tsp fine sea salt [2.4%]
- 5 g / 1 tsp fennel seeds (optional) [1%]
- 400 g / 1 ⅔ cups water [80%]
- 256 g / 1 ¼ cup starter (from Day 1) [51%]

Day 2: At 7:00 PM, combine all the dry ingredients for the dough in a large bowl. Add the water and starter and mix well. Stretch and fold the dough (see page 40) every 20 minutes for 1 ½ hours. Cover and place the dough in the fridge overnight.

Day 3: 12–15 hours later, remove the dough from the fridge.

Dust a banneton or proofing basket with flour.

Shape the dough into a bâtard (oval). Place the shaped dough in the proofing basket and allow to ferment at room temperature for 2 hours.

Preheat the oven and the Dutch oven at 450°F.

Bake, covered, for 35 minutes. Remove the lid and bake for an additional 25–30 minutes. Allow to cool on a rack before slicing.

Pain au Levain (a.k.a. Traditional French Sourdough)

After baking through the night and most of the morning, we finally sat down for a much-needed repast. A simple lunch of asparagus (always with Gérard's beloved hazelnut or walnut oil and a sprinkling of salt), hard cheese, French salami, and, of course, freshly baked bread and Vermont butter. We savoured the food in silence, exhausted from the many hours of baking.

"I think you are ready to learn about the levain," Gérard suddenly stated. "Yes, I think so. Tomorrow we start. Make sure you bring your notebook and pen with you in the morning. Good night." It was only half past four in the afternoon, but that was his way. The schedule of a baker. The dance of the levain.

I cleared the table and mused to myself. Ready to learn about the levain? Ready to make my very own traditional French stiff-dough sourdough starter? This was most exciting. And a great honour in itself, as Gérard usually reserved the secrets of the levain for the very end of the apprenticeship program, many months down the line. But there I was, two weeks deep in the dough, my reality about to be changed forever.

Over the next week, Gérard guided me in the process of creating a young levain. Freshly milled rye and spelt flours were meticulously combined with water and a touch of malt powder—just enough to encourage the wild yeasts in the whole-grain flour to start working their own magic.

The young starter needed to be checked on and fed regularly, often causing me to return to the bakery at midnight or the wee hours of the morning. My waking hours were filled with thoughts of the levain. Was the starter happy? Was it healthy? What could I do to help it along? Many a night I woke in a mild panic, worried I had forgotten to feed the starter or that something had gone horribly wrong. Yet the sleepless nights paid off and the starter proved a success.

Gérard, however, was not convinced, calling it "beginner's luck." He instructed me to create a second starter following the same approach. Much to his surprise (or horror), the second starter also took off and soon I was juggling two starters and feeding them at various intervals throughout the day (and night!). This only exacerbated the baker's annoyance. He then directed me to get rid of one of the starters, stressing that multitasking is a recipe for disaster. It was with a heavy heart that I discarded the second levain, keeping the first and naming her "Maggie" after the baker's girlfriend, a woman of immense creativity, character, and spirit.

A decade later in 2023, Gérard and Maggie have both passed on, yet their legacy remains, preserved in the namesake sourdough starter I took from Vermont to South Africa and now all the way to Canada. Over the years, I have shared the starter with many friends, students, and bakers. Versions of her are now happily baking away in the US, Canada, South Africa, France, Greece, Italy, and Spain.

The Apprentice Loaf

Gérard Rubaud was old school. He favoured quality over quantity. "Do not overcomplicate things by offering too many different breads," he advised. "Choose one or two types of bread, but make them really well." Sage advice and applicable to more than just baking.

The Apprentice Loaf was designed to teach Gérard's apprentices the ropes. A practice loaf of sorts. Once the novice bakers had proven themselves, the apprentice loaves were sold to the local stores on consignment. The loaves were baked in a large masonry oven, fed by wood from Gérard's own forest, giving them extra character and charm.

NOTE: You can easily substitute the spelt for another whole-grain flour such as Kamut, Red Fife wheat, or even dark rye. While an authentic pain au levain is leavened with a stiff starter, you can also use a liquid sourdough starter, though I recommend reducing the amount of water in the final dough a little, to 375 g / 1 ½ cups.

NOTE: The 30 g / ⅛ cup of levain that is not added to the dough can be kept in a jar and maintained as a stiff starter. To feed or grow the starter, dissolve 25–30 g / ⅛ cup of levain in 30 g / ¼ cup water. Add 50 g / ¼ cup of all-purpose or bread flour and a pinch of salt and work it into a smooth dough. Place in a jar and allow to rise for 8–10 hours before using it in a recipe, or place in the fridge. Alternatively, the blob of starter may be used up in a "discard recipe," given to a friend, or simply thrown out.

MAKES 2 SMALL LOAVES

Day 1: Levain

15 g / 1 Tbsp liquid sourdough starter (ripe)
40 g / ¼ cup water
75 g / ¾ cup all-purpose or unbleached white bread flour
1 small pinch of salt

In a small bowl, dissolve the starter in the water. Add the flour and pinch of salt and knead until smooth, then shape into a ball. Cover and allow to rise in a cozy (but not overly hot place) overnight (8–10 hours).

Day 2: Dough

400 g / 3 ¼ cups all-purpose or unbleached white bread flour [80%]
100 g / ¾ cup spelt flour (preferably freshly milled) [20%]
410 g / 1 ¾ cups water (lukewarm) [82%]
100 g / ½ cup levain (from Day 1) [20%]
11 g / 1 ¾ tsp fine sea salt [2.2%]

Combine the flours and water in a large bowl. Cover and set aside for approximately 30 minutes (called an autolyse, see page 37). Observe the dough mixture after the autolyse. It should have relaxed considerably.

Break or cut 100 g / ½ cup of the levain into smaller pieces and distribute them equally across the surface of the dough. Gently stretch and fold the dough over itself (see page 40), incorporating the levain and working the gluten strands. Cover and allow to rest for 15 minutes.

Sprinkle the salt over the surface of the dough, then gently work it in. Cover and set aside for 1 hour. Return to the dough and perform a few stretches and folds. Repeat twice more over the next 2 hours.

After the third hour's stretch and fold, allow the dough to rise for an additional hour.

When the dough has fermented for a total of 4 hours, gently tip it out onto a countertop lightly dusted with flour. Fold the dough over itself 2–3 times but take care not to deflate it. Divide the dough in half and pre-shape into loose rounds. Cover with a kitchen towel and allow to rest for 30 minutes.

Prepare containers for the final rise of the dough. You can use a well-floured banneton or bread basket, a large sheet of parchment paper, or a couche (in which the dough will rise in the folds).

Shape each piece of dough into a bâtard (oval) and place them seam-side up into the bread basket or other surface. Cover and allow for a final rise of 2–3 hours.

Preheat the oven (and the cast iron Dutch oven, if using) to 450°F. (If you have 2 Dutch ovens, the loaves can be baked simultaneously. Alternatively, one loaf can rest in the fridge (covered) while the other is being baked.)

Gently transfer the risen dough to a sheet of parchment paper (just big enough for the dough to comfortably fit). If the dough proofed in the folds of a sheet of parchment paper, the paper can be pulled sideways (to the left and right) so as to flatten the crease/fold. Using a pair of scissors, cut along the same fold so that you have two separate pieces of parchment each carrying a piece of dough. Lifting the paper, transfer the dough into the Dutch oven and score the surface of the dough. Bake in the preheated oven, covered, for 30 minutes. Remove the lid and bake for an additional 20–25 minutes or until beautifully golden and caramelized.

Cooksmart

Gérard's Sourdough (Pain au Levain)

This loaf was the baker's masterpiece. Large and robust, with Gérard's signature scoring pattern of an ear of wheat, it was a magnificent loaf indeed and one of the best breads I have ever eaten. Gérard preferred an even crumb with small-to-medium-sized bubbles and was not at all impressed by the "rockstar" bakers who push their dough and hydration percentages to the limit. "Who wants to have their marmalade dripping onto their lap whilst eating breakfast? Non, merci!" Naturally, the best French toast is made with French sourdough, so be sure to reserve a few slices and whip up a batch of Gérard's pain perdu (page 250) for a special weekend breakfast!

NOTE: Baking in a Dutch oven helps beginner bakers produce neater, more consistent loaves. But if you prefer a more rustic look, you can bake both the Apprentice Loaf (page 138) and this one on a baking sheet lined with parchment paper using a good amount of steam. (Note that it will be harder to control the steam and expansion of the dough.)

Gérard's bread usually sold out within fifteen minutes of being delivered to the local stores. With its soft, buttery crumb and smooth crust (Gérard did not approve of sharp ears on the crust) this loaf was made for everyday eating.

MAKES 1 LARGE LOAF

Day 1: Levain

15 g / 1 Tbsp liquid sourdough starter (ripe)
40 g / ¼ cup water
75 g / ¾ cup all-purpose or unbleached white bread flour
1 small pinch of salt

In a small mixing bowl, dilute the starter in the water and mix in the flour. On a lightly floured counter, knead until smooth, then shape into a ball. Cover and allow it to rise in a cozy (but not overly hot) place overnight (8–10 hours).

Day 2: Dough

450 g /3 ¾ cup all-purpose or unbleached white bread flour [90%]
50 g / ¼ cup spelt [10%]
400 g / 1 ¾ cups water (lukewarm) [80%]
100 g levain (from Day 1) [20%]
13 g / 2 ¼ tsp salt [2.6%]

Combine the flours and water in a large bowl. Cover and set aside for at least 30 minutes.

Add 100 g / ½ cup of levain and gently work it into the dough mixture. Once the lumps have disappeared, cover and set aside for 10–15 minutes.

Sprinkle the salt across the surface of the dough and gently fold it in. Cover and set aside for 1 hour.

Give the dough a stretch and fold (see page 40), to strengthen the dough, as usual, but also to distribute the salt, since its addition is delayed in doughs made with an autolyse. Allow the dough to bulk ferment for a total of 4 hours, giving it a few stretches and folds after every hour. (Remember that it may take even longer in winter).

After the fourth hour of fermentation, do not stretch and fold the dough. Instead, tip it out onto a lightly floured work surface and pre-shape it into a loose round. Cover the dough and set aside for 30 minutes.

Shape the dough into a bâtard (see page 46) and place it seam-side up in a floured banneton or proofing basket, a couche, or between the folds of a sheet of parchment paper. Allow the dough to proof for 3–4 hours, until well risen, light, and puffy.

Preheat the oven (and, if using, the cast iron Dutch oven) to 450°F.

Score the dough with a sharp blade or baker's lame. Bake, covered, for 30 minutes. Remove the lid and bake for an additional 15–20 minutes or until beautifully golden and caramelized.

Greek Village Bread (Horiatiko Psomi)

Village bread, country bread, and *pain de campagne* are only a few examples of staple breads that not too long ago still nourished whole communities. And although the ingredients (and methods) may vary from one culture or region to the next, the reference to a pastoral, rural, rustic way of life is undeniable. This is the bread my late father-in-law, Ioannis Kourelos, remembered with great fondness. It remains one of the most popular breads in Greece even today, though many modern versions are now made with baker's yeast instead of sourdough.

NOTE: This recipe can easily be doubled to produce a larger, more traditional-looking loaf.

MAKES 1 LARGE LOAF

Day 1: Levain (2 options)

Feed the stiff starter (if you have one) or use your liquid starter to make a stiff starter for this recipe.

Stiff starter

25–30 g / ⅛ cup stiff starter (levain)
40 g / ¼ cup water (lukewarm)
50 g / ½ cup all-purpose or unbleached white bread flour
Pinch of fine sea salt

Liquid starter

15 g / 1 Tbsp liquid sourdough starter (ripe)
40 g / ¼ cup water
75 g / ¾ cup all-purpose or unbleached white bread flour

If you have some stiff starter from a previous bake, you can feed the levain as per the instructions for feeding the stiff starter.

Alternatively, in a small bowl, dilute the liquid starter in the water and add the flour. Work into a smooth dough, then shape into a round. Cover, and allow to rise in a cozy place overnight (8–10 hours).

Day 2: Dough

450 g / 3 ¾ cups all-purpose or white bread flour [90%]
50 g / ¼ cup fine semolina flour [10%]
10 g / 1 ¾ tsp fine sea salt [2%]
320 g / 1 ¼ cups water (lukewarm) [64%]
20 g / 1 Tbsp honey [4%]
15 g / 1 Tbsp olive oil [3%]
15 g / 1 Tbsp milk [3%]
80 g levain (either option) [16%]

Heavy, round, and decidedly robust, these loaves would traditionally have been leavened with sourdough and baked in large wood-fired ovens. They stem from a time when bread truly was the staff of life—the sustenance that enabled long hours of toil on the land. The food that built civilizations. The village oven, often referred to as a communal oven, was a place of gathering. Long before every household boasted its own oven, communities would congregate around a shared hearth to bake their weekly bread and slow-cook meat and other dishes.

In a mixing bowl, combine the bread flour, fine semolina flour, and salt. Slowly add the liquid ingredients and work into a soft dough. This is not a wet dough, but it should not be too dry either. (Do not be afraid to add a few tablespoons of water if the dough is feeling dry or hard.)

Measure out 80 g of the ripe levain (stiff starter) and reserve (so as to maintain) or discard the remainder. Cut the starter into smaller pieces and dot the pieces across the surface of the dough before gently but thoroughly mixing them into the dough). Cover and allow to rise for 5–6 hours. Perform a few stretches and folds (see page 40) every hour or so throughout the bulk fermentation.

Line a baking sheet with parchment paper.

Tip the dough out onto a lightly floured surface and shape into a large boule (round). Place onto the prepared baking sheet and lightly push down to flatten the dough slightly. Cover with a damp kitchen towel and allow it to rise for an additional 3–4 hours.

Preheat the oven to 425°F. This bread requires plenty of steam. (See page 53 for options to create steam.) If you are baking on a baking sheet and using the pan method to create steam, preheat the pan/skillet as the oven preheats and have a small bowl of ice on hand. If using a cast iron Dutch oven, preheat the pot while the oven is preheating.

Brush the surface of the dough with a little water and sprinkle with sesame seeds. Score the dough with a sharp knife or baker's lame. Bake in the preheated oven, with steam for 20 minutes. Remove the skillet of steaming water and bake for an additional 25–30 minutes until beautifully golden. If using a Dutch oven, gently lift the dough with the parchment paper into the pot. Remove the lid after 25–30 minutes and continue baking for 20 minutes or until beautifully golden.

GOLDEN SYRUP
ABRAM LYLE & SONS
SUGAR REFINERS
454g ℮
PARTIALLY INVERTED REFINERS SYRUP

Sourdough Sandwich Bread

Although the chapter on straight dough breads offers a great many options for sandwich breads, a sourdough version is not to be missed. As a general rule, it helps to reduce the hydration of sandwich loaves, as a slightly firmer dough is much easier to handle and shape than a soft, bubbly, high-hydration dough. As such, any of the above sourdough recipes can be used to make a wonderful sandwich bread simply by reducing the amount of water/liquid in the dough to roughly 70 percent. This means for a dough containing 500 g of flour, use approximately 350 g of water/liquid.

I recommend using a 13 × 4 × 4-inch Pullman pan (with lid) or any similar sized pan of your choice. If making two smaller loaves, two 8 × 4-inch loaf pans will also work well.

MAKES 1 LARGE LOAF

- 1 batch sourdough bread dough prepared with 70% hydration (350 g water to 500 g flour)

Grease the bread pan, and if using a Pullman pan, make sure to grease the inside of the lid too.

When the dough has bulk fermented for 5 hours, gently tip it out onto a lightly floured work surface. Dust the dough with a little flour and roll it out into a rectangle the length of your bread tin. Roll the dough up into a tight roll and place it seam-side down into the prepared pan. Close the lid or loosely cover the dough with cling film or a damp kitchen towel and allow to rise for 2–2 ½ hours.

NOTE: If you use a Pullman pan, the dough may be placed in the fridge after shaping and left to rest overnight. The loaf can be baked straight from the fridge the next day and does not need to come to room temperature.

Preheat the oven to 440°F or the maximum temperature recommended by the manufacturer of the Pullman pan (temperatures vary from one brand to the next). This bread requires steam. (See page 53 for options to create steam.) If you are using the pan method, preheat the pan/skillet as the oven preheats and have a bowl of ice cubes on hand. The Pullman pans require no additional steam.

If you're not using a Pullman pan, score the dough with a sharp knife or baker's lame. If using a Pullman pan, remove the lid after 30 minutes and continue to bake for an additional 20–25 minutes. If not using a Pullman pan, bake with steam for 20–25 minutes then remove the skillet that the water is in (or stop spraying). Continue to bake for 15–20 minutes until golden brown.

Remove from the bread tin and allow to cool on a wire rack. For a softer crust, the hot bread may be wrapped in a clean kitchen towel until cooled completely.

NOTE: A normal loaf pan may also be placed inside a large Dutch oven (or on a baking sheet and covered by an inverted pot / stainless steel bowl) to simulate the steamy conditions created when baking in a Pullman pan—though this method will not yield the same square-shaped loaf.

It is Sunday morning and I am in my kitchen in Kensington, Johannesburg, slicing bread (rather noisily, I might add). My family is coming over for a braai (BBQ) today and I am making braaibroodjies. This loaf has been sitting on the counter for a few days and it is fighting back, its chewy, leathery crust creaking and splintering as the long-bladed bread knife mercilessly tears through the (surprisingly still quite delicate) crumb. As scraps of bread and crust tumble to the floor, I look down. Tango and Cash, our two Smooth Fox Terriers, are at my feet, their undocked tails wagging with excitement. They love sourdough, especially the crusty bits! I think of Gérard and his chocolate Labradors. "Humans have become out of touch," I recall him saying. "But animals," he continued, "animals instinctively recognize real food. You can place a slice of authentic sourdough and a slice of store-bought bread in front of a dog, and it will instinctively go for the sourdough."

Kitke (Challah) 155
Milk Bread 157
Hot Cross Buns 160
Raisin Bread with Cinnamon & Aniseed 163
Cinnamon Buns 164
Marzipan Stollen 167

Sweet & Enriched Breads

Fats and sugars, when transformed into baked goods, are our ultimate indulgence, guilty pleasures that have the ability to comfort, console, and—according to American chef and cookbook author Christina Tosi—save the world. When added to a bread dough, these ingredients enrich and elevate the resulting loaves. Think soft, fluffy, and wonderfully airy challahs, chocolate babkas, jam doughnuts, and cinnamon buns—happiness in every bite!

Breads that contain dairy, eggs, fats, oils, and sugars are referred to as enriched breads. These enrichments yield loaves with softer crusts and beautifully tender crumbs. Sandwich breads, celebration breads, soft dinner rolls, and braided breads are examples of loaves usually made with an enriched dough. Enriched breads can be used for extra-special French toast or bread puddings.

Enrichments do, however, play havoc with the fermentation of the dough, often necessitating significantly longer fermentation times. The type and quantity of the enrichment affects the dough in different ways.

Sugar can slow down the fermentation because it absorbs some of the moisture/liquid in the dough and the yeast has to work harder to become properly hydrated before it can start its feeding and the fermentation can begin.

Fat (eggs, oil, butter, dairy) can impede fermentation as they can coat the flour. This results in the yeast taking longer to reach and eventually consume the simple sugars within the flour (carbohydrates).

All of this means the dough will need enough time to ferment so the yeast can properly work its way through. Whatever you do, do not rush an enriched dough! Once the dough has successfully undergone the bulk fermentation period, it can be portioned and shaped as desired.

I am not going to peddle you another recipe for brioche or the ever-popular croissant. Baked delights that, although leavened with yeast, actually fall under pastry or viennoiserie rather than bread and often cause the home baker (especially the novice baker) more trouble than the results are worth. Leave those for the professional pastry chefs. Instead, try your hand at the simple, downright moreish sweet dough recipes tucked away in these pages.

In this chapter you will discover a selection of versatile recipes as well as ideas on how to have fun with your dough, swapping out one ingredient for another or using the same dough to produce a range of different treats. Remember, delicious does not have to mean complicated. More often than not, the simplest and most unassuming recipes come out on top.

Despite their deliciousness and immense popularity, sweet and enriched loaves are definitely not everyday breads. Traditionally, these breads and their luxurious ingredients were reserved for religious and celebratory occasions and, of course, the wealthy elite. Below you will find two of my favourite enriched dough recipes and a few notes on how to tweak them to produce a multitude of delicious variations. And as an added bonus I offer my go-to recipe for Marzipan Stollen (page 167), with homemade marzipan of course!

My sisters and I had our very first taste of sweet and enriched bread at a Saint Nicholas Day festival in Germany. The Stutenkerl or Weckmann is a sweet dough bread formed and baked in the shape of a man (usually sporting a clay pipe). This celebration bread is beautifully soft, with a subtle hint of citrus zest.

Wilton
15.25 x 10.25 x .75 in

Kitke (Challah)

Humans have been braiding bread for centuries. Beautifully plaited loaves are found within the culinary traditions of many different cultures, often steeped in religious symbolism or accompanied by intriguing folklore and rituals. Baked for special occasions and holidays, the Jewish challah is known and loved by many. In South Africa, this bread is also known as *kitke*, an archaic Yiddish word that points to the Lithuanian origins of many Jewish immigrants. Sadly, this unique moniker is in danger of falling out of use, as younger generations are adopting the more commonly used *challah*.

NOTE: Traditional kitke contains no dairy and is sweetened with honey rather than sugar. Some recipes also call for 4 yolks instead of 2 whole eggs, or 2 eggs and 2 yolks.

SUBSTITUTION: Try swapping the oil in this recipe for butter and the water for warm milk to yield a bread similar to the German Hefezopf. Adding a little orange or lemon zest to the milk and butter dough will bring it closer to an Italian or even Ukrainian Easter bread. And if you were to add mahlepi and mastiha or aniseed into the mix, you will end up with the dough for Greek tsoureki.

MAKES 2 MEDIUM KITKE

Dough

500 g / 4 cups white bread flour [100%]
8 g / 2 ¼ tsp instant yeast [1.6%]
30–35 g sugar [6–7%] or 60g honey* [12%]
10 g / 1 ¾ tsp fine sea salt [2%]
2 eggs (beaten)
45 g mild olive oil or sunflower oil [9%]
180–230 g / 1 cup water (lukewarm) [36–46%] (the hydration % depends on the type of flour used)

Egg wash and topping

1 egg yolk (beaten, for the egg wash)
15 g / 3 tsp water (lukewarm)
Sesame seeds, poppy seeds, flaked almonds, or pearl sugar (all optional)

**If using honey, be extra conservative with the water!*

Combine the flour, yeast, sugar (if using), and salt in a large bowl. Add the honey (if using), beaten eggs, oil, and water and mix together. Be very careful not to add too much water, only enough to bring it together into a soft, sticky dough that is not overly wet. (An overly hydrated dough results in a braid that will be somewhat flat instead of voluptuous and curvy.) Knead the dough on a countertop until smooth. (After a few minutes of kneading, the dough should become less sticky and more manageable. Add flour conservatively and only if the dough remains sticky after 5–10 minutes of kneading.) Cover and allow the dough to rise for 2–3 hours, kneading again briefly after every hour. (**NOTE:** In winter and on cold and overcast days, the bulk fermentation time may be even longer, as the cold will further slow the yeast activity.)

Line a baking sheet with parchment paper.

Divide the dough into 6 equal pieces and shape (roll) each piece into a log 10–12 inches long. To shape the kitke, braid 3 strands together, starting from the middle and working downward. Pinch the ends together and tuck them under to neaten. Turn the half plait around and continue braiding.

Seal the ends together, tuck them under, then place the braided loaves on the prepared baking sheet.

Brush the loaves with egg wash and invert a large plastic container or ceramic dish over each braid to prevent them from drying out. Alternatively, place a large freezer bag loosely over the top of each braid. Allow to rise for 60–80 minutes or until plump and almost doubled.

Preheat the oven to 400°F.

Carefully brush the loaves with egg wash again before topping with seeds, almonds, or sugar. Bake in the preheated oven for 20–25 minutes until the braids are a deep reddish-golden brown. If browning too quickly, lay a sheet of tinfoil loosely over the top and continue baking. Allow to cool on a wire rack.

Variations

GERMAN HEFEZOPF

Milk and butter dough (instead of oil and water). Flaked almonds for the topping.

UKRAINIAN PASKA BREAD

Milk and butter dough (instead of oil and water) plus the zest of half an orange and half a lemon and a simple powdered sugar and water/milk icing.

ITALIAN EASTER BREAD

Milk and butter dough (instead of oil and water) plus the zest of one orange and a dyed egg. A simple powdered sugar and water/milk icing is also common.

GREEK TSOUREKI

Milk and butter dough (instead of oil and water) plus:

5 g / 1 ¼ tsp mahlepi or mahleb*
1 g / ¼ tsp ground mastiha or mastic**
Zest of 1 orange
1 red dyed egg
Optional extras: 1g / ¼ tsp ground cardamom
or aniseed

**A spice with a strong bitter cherry and almond flavour made from finely ground cherry seeds, commonly used in Greek and Middle Eastern foods, especially bread and desserts.*

***A plant resin used in Greek and Mediterranean cuisine.*

Milk Bread

Milk breads are universally popular, though the ingredients and methods used to produce them differ from one country to the next. The French pain au lait is vastly different from Turkish milk bread, which again is unlike Chinese and Japanese milk breads, though they all share the same name and similar ingredients.

This recipe calls for a pre-cooked paste of flour and milk called *tangzhong*. Pre-cooking a portion of the flour causes the starch to gelatinize, which in turn contributes to a light, fluffy, and exceptionally airy bread.

NOTE: This dough is beautifully versatile and can be used to make hamburger or hot dog rolls, doughnuts, cinnamon buns, and more!

When making a large milk bread, I always turn to the large Pullman pan (13 × 4 × 4-inch). Whereas 8 ½-inch pans work well when making two smaller loaves.

MAKES 1 LARGE OR 2 SMALL MILK BREADS

Tangzhong

150 g / ½ cup full-fat milk [30%]
30 g / ½ cup white bread flour [6%]

Main Dough

470 g / 3 ½ cups white bread flour [94%]
70 g / ¼ cup caster sugar [14%]
5 g / ¾ tsp fine sea salt [1%]
10 g / 3 tsp instant yeast [2%]
Tangzhong (see above)
150 g / ½ cup milk (lukewarm) [30%]
1 egg
80 g / ¼ cup unsalted butter (softened but not melted) [16%]

Egg Wash

15 g milk or 1 egg and 15g cream / plain yogurt or 15 g / ¾ Tbsp condensed milk

Pour the milk into a small pot and gently warm it over low heat. Slowly add the flour, stirring constantly with a wooden spoon or silicone spatula. Once the mixture has thickened to a paste, remove from the heat and allow to cool until lukewarm. This is your tangzhong!

Add the remaining dry ingredients to a large bowl (or the bowl of a stand mixer) and mix briefly. In a separate bowl, whisk together the tangzhong, remaining milk, and 1 egg. Add the wet ingredients to the dry ingredients and work into a basic dough. Slowly add cubes of the softened butter into the dough and mix until all the butter is incorporated. Transfer the dough to a lightly floured work surface and knead until smooth. Avoid adding additional flour, as this will change the texture of the final loaf. Instead, use the dough scraper to control the dough and scrape the counter as necessary.

Once the dough is smooth, shape it into a ball and place it in a clean bowl. Cover and allow it to rest for 1 hour. Gently stretch and fold the dough (see page 40), then cover and set aside for an additional hour.

Line a loaf pan with parchment paper.

Divide the dough into 3 equal pieces for a single loaf, 6 pieces for 2 loaves, and 4 pieces for a Pullman pan. Using a rolling pin, roll each piece into an oval approximately 6–8 inches long. Roll the dough up tightly and place 3 pieces into each pan or 4 pieces into the Pullman pan. Cover the dough loosely with clingfilm and allow to rise for 1–1 ¼ hours.

Preheat the oven to 350°F.

Brush the dough with the egg wash of your choice. For this recipe, there is no need to use the lid of the Pullman pan. Bake a large loaf for 30–35 minutes or 2 smaller loaves for 25 minutes. Cool on a wire rack before tearing the segments apart. Enjoy!

As Socrates said, "Everything in moderation. Nothing in excess." When we were children, we had sugary treats only on the weekend and special occasions—joyful highlights rather than everyday affairs. To this day, I am thankful to my mother for setting a healthy example for us with food. She made wholesome, nutritious, homemade meals the norm. My sisters and I came to appreciate sugary treats as occasional delights, something to look forward to, to savour and relish. Unsurprisingly, the habit of moderate sugar consumption carried over into my baking routine, where sweet bakes feature few and far between.

Hot Cross Buns

A good hot cross bun makes for a beautiful Easter weekend. But do not skimp on the spices—nobody likes a bland bun! It is perfectly acceptable to enjoy these fragrant buns with a scandalous amount of butter. They are a fabulously flavourful addition to your Easter baking repertoire. Enjoy on Good Friday as per the English Easter tradition.

NOTE: This dough can also be used to make a delicious sandwich loaf, perfect for uniform slices and lunchbox treats. One batch of dough will easily fill a large Pullman pan. Alternatively, use two 8 × 4-inch loaf pans. Grease the pans, shape the dough into ovals, and allow to rise for 60–80 minutes before baking.

MAKES 12 BUNS

150 g / ¾ cup mix of raisins / sultanas / mixed peel
23 g / 3 Tbsp ground cinnamon [4.6%]
2 g / ¾ tsp ground cloves [0.4%]
500 g / 4 cups bread flour
50 g / ¼ cup caster sugar [10%]
5 g / ¾ tsp salt [1%]
10 g / 4 ½ tsp instant yeast [2%]
1 egg
45 g / ¼ cup butter (melted) or sunflower oil [9%]
230–250 g / 1 cup milk or water (lukewarm) [46–50%]

Egg wash

1 egg yolk
2 Tbsp water

Crosses

80 g / ⅝ cup all-purpose flour
13 g / 1 Tbsp caster sugar
80–85 g / ¼ cup water
Butter (melted) for brushing (optional)

Combine the dried fruit mixture in a small bowl, with water to cover, and set aside to soak.

Add the spices to the dry ingredients and prepare the dough as per the kitke recipe (page 155).

After the first hour of bulk fermentation, drain the raisin mixture in a sieve and scatter the fruit over the dough. Gently work the dough until all the fruit has been incorporated. Cover and allow to rise for an additional 60–80 minutes.

Line a quarter or half sheet pan with parchment paper.

Divide the dough into 12 equal pieces. You can either eye-ball it or weigh the dough. To do this, remove the dough from the bowl, "zero" or tare the scale, then place the dough on the scale. Divide the number shown on the scale by 12. Portion the dough accordingly, using a bench scraper, sharp knife, or the straight side of a dough scraper. If the dough is too sticky to handle dust very lightly with flour. Shape into rounds and place in the prepared pan. (If you want the buns to rise into each other, place them relatively close to each other. For individual round buns, leave approximately 1–1 ½ inches between each bun.) Cover and allow to rise for 60–80 minutes. Don't rush the dough. Allow the buns to at least double in size before moving on to the next step.

Preheat the oven to 400°F.

In a small bowl, beat the egg yolk and water together for the egg wash.

Combine the flour, sugar, and water for the crosses and place the mixture in a piping bag. Brush the buns with the egg wash then pipe crosses over them.

Bake on the middle rack of the preheated oven for 18–20 minutes, or until golden and cooked through. (The buns should be soft and bouncy, not dry or hard to the touch.) Brush the hot buns with the melted butter (if using) and allow to cool on a cooling rack. Store them in an airtight container.

Raisin Bread with Cinnamon & Aniseed

Growing up, my sisters and I loved the Enid Blyton books. We spent many a weekend and holiday absorbed in the adventures of *The Secret Seven* and *The Famous Five*. In addition to the mysteries and exciting quests, I thoroughly enjoyed reading about the children's afternoon tea. The intrepid adventurers frequently sat down to scrumptious picnics in the beautiful English countryside! Much like the Blyton stories, this raisin loaf is charming, if a little old-fashioned. Serve it fresh or toasted with plenty of butter or use it as a base for a beautifully fragrant bread pudding. Enjoy!

MAKES 1 LARGE LOAF (OR 12 BUNS)

80 g / ½ cup raisins [16%]
1 batch Government Loaf (page 67), Kitke (page 155), or Milk Bread (page 157) dough
2.6 g / 1 tsp cinnamon [0.5%]
1 g / ½ tsp ground aniseed [0.2%]

In a small bowl, soak the raisins in the water or cold rooibos tea and set aside.

Follow the instructions in your chosen dough recipe, adding the spices in with the dry ingredients.

After 1 hour of fermentation, drain the soaked raisins in a sieve, sprinkle them over the dough, and gently work them in until well incorporated. Cover the dough and allow it to rest for an additional hour.

Shape the dough into a large loaf or 12 small buns. Loosely cover the dough and allow it to rise for 60–80 minutes, until doubled.

Preheat the oven to 390°F.

Bake for 30–35 minutes for a large loaf and 15–20 minutes for the rolls, until beautifully golden and cooked through (should sound hollow when tapped underneath). Transfer to a rack to cool.

Cinnamon Buns

Freshly baked cinnamon buns are one of life's greatest joys. These soft, fluffy, melt-in-your-mouth buns are easy to make and a guaranteed crowd pleaser! As an added bonus, they freeze well and can quickly be defrosted for a fantastic midweek breakfast treat or lunchbox surprise. Both the Kitke dough (page 155) and the Milk Bread dough (page 157) yield fantastic, super-soft buns, but remember to allow the enriched dough sufficient time to rise, or you may end up with rather lacklustre buns. I recommend making a double batch, as these disappear quickly!

VARIATIONS: This dough can also be baked as a cinnamon swirl loaf. Simply seal off the seams and place the dough in a greased Pullman pan. Allow to rise for 60–80 minutes. Bake for 30–35 minutes at 380°F. Remove the lid and bake for an additional 10–15 minutes. Gently release from the pan and allow to cool on a wire rack.

Both the Kitke and Milk Bread doughs can be used to make exquisite chocolate babkas or extra fancy dinner rolls. They can also be filled with many other delicious ingredients. Think dark chocolate chips and pistachio nuts, or milk chocolate chips and coconut flakes. Savoury fillings work equally well, like a roasted garlic and aged cheddar loaf or a basil pesto and parmesan bread.

MAKES 6 LARGE CINNAMON BUNS

1 batch Kitke (page 155) or Milk Bread (page 157) dough

Filling

50 g / 4 Tbsp caster sugar
12 g / 4 tsp cinnamon
60 g / ½ cup butter (softened)

Icing

250 g / 2 cups icing sugar
30–60 g / 2–4 Tbsp milk or water

Prepare the dough as per the chosen recipe. Allow for a bulk fermentation time of 2–3 hours.

Combine the sugar and cinnamon in a small bowl.

Line a baking sheet with parchment paper.

On a lightly floured surface, roll the dough out into a large rectangle about 8 × 12 inches. Combine the softened butter and cinnamon sugar and mix into a thick paste. (Reserve a little for sprinkling over the buns prior to baking.) Using a plastic dough scraper or a spatula, spread the mixture evenly over the surface of the dough. Roll up into a log lengthwise and seal the seam with your fingers or the palm of your hand. Turn the log over so that the seam is at the bottom.

Slice the log into 6 equal discs and place the spirals on the prepared baking sheet. If you want the rolls to rise into each other (pull-apart buns), place them closer together. For individual cinnamon rolls, allow sufficient space (1–1 ½ inches) between the dough spirals. Cover and allow to rise for 60–80 minutes.

Preheat the oven to 390°F.

Sprinkle the remaining cinnamon sugar over the top of the rolls. Bake pull-apart buns for 20–25 minutes, until the edges are golden and make sure that the buns at the very centre are baked through! Bake the individual buns for 15–20 minutes. The cinnamon buns should be beautifully golden and springy/bouncy to the touch. Allow to cool on a wire rack.

Combine the icing sugar and milk or water into a thick mixture. Be careful not to add too much liquid, as the icing will be too runny and translucent. Use a spoon or spatula to drizzle the icing over the cooled buns. Enjoy with a good cup of coffee!

NOTE: Cream cheese frosting makes for a delicious alternative to the simple sugar glaze.

Marzipan Stollen

When I was ten years old, we lived in Cologne, Germany, for a year. My sisters and I attended a German school, and by the time we returned to South Africa we spoke fluent German. Besides picking up an additional language, we also developed a taste for Berliner (page 212) and marzipan stollen. Packed with fruit, nuts, and homemade marzipan, stollen makes a wonderful addition to the Christmas table and is great for gifting too! It is traditional to soak the fruit in rum or brandy, but orange juice or rooibos tea make excellent substitutions.

MAKES 1 LARGE OR 2 SMALL STOLLEN

Day 1: Fruit soaker

130 g / ¾ cup raisins
130 g / ¾ cup sultanas
60 g / ⅔ cup mixed peel
60 g / ¼ cup glace cherries (roughly chopped)
Rum, brandy, orange juice, or rooibos tea (for soaking)

In a bowl, combine the fruit, citrus peel, and rum or brandy (for a non-alcoholic version, use orange juice or cold rooibos tea). Stir the mixture well, cover, and allow it to rest overnight.

Day 2: Dough

500 g / 4 cups white bread or all-purpose flour [100%]
12 g / 2 tsp instant yeast [2.4%]
75 g / ⅓ cup caster sugar [15%]
8 g / 1 ¼ tsp fine sea salt [1.6%]
8 g / 1 ½ tsp cinnamon [1.6%]
Zest of ½ lemon / 1 tsp
Zest of ½ orange / 1 tsp
125 g / ½ cup milk (lukewarm) [25%]
215 g / 1 cup unsalted butter [43%]
2 eggs
5 g / 1 ¼ tsp vanilla extract [1%]
100 g / 1 ¼ cups flaked almonds [20%] (optional)

Marzipan (or use store bought)

200 g / 1 ¾ cups ground almonds
100 g ¾ cup icing sugar (for sweeter marzipan, add an additional 100 g icing sugar)
5 g / 1 tsp almond extract or rose water (food grade)
45 g / ¼ cup water or lemon juice

Topping

150 g / ¾ cup butter (melted)
150 g / 1 ¼ cups icing sugar

Add all the dry ingredients to a large bowl and stir briefly.

In a medium bowl, whisk together the milk, butter, eggs, vanilla extract, and the zests.

Add the liquid ingredients to the flour mixture and combine into a dough. Knead on a lightly floured surface for a few minutes, until the dough is smooth. Cover and set aside for 30 minutes.

Drain the fruit mixture from Day 1 in a sieve then scatter the fruit and flaked almonds (if using) over the surface of the dough. Gently work the fruit and nuts into the dough by hand. Cover and leave the dough to rise for 2–3 hours, with a stretch and fold (see page 40) after the first and second hour.

While the dough is rising, prepare the marzipan. Combine the ground almonds, icing sugar, almond extract (or rose water), and water (or lemon juice) in a blender and pulse until the ingredients come together into a firm dough. (NOTE: It is possible to mix the marzipan by hand, but the texture will not be as smooth as marzipan created in a blender.) If the marzipan is too dry, add a little more water or lemon juice.

Line one large or two small baking sheets with parchment paper.

Tip the dough out onto a floured surface and divide it into 2 equal pieces. Gently pull/stretch the dough so it resembles a small rectangle/oval (10–12 inches long). Place a log of marzipan (the length of the dough) in the centre of each piece of dough and fold the dough over itself to enclose the marzipan. Gently but firmly seal the seams with your fingers or the base of your palm. Transfer to the prepared baking sheet(s) with the seams at the bottom and allow to rise for a further 60 minutes, or until doubled.

Preheat the oven to 350°F.

Bake the loaves for 40–50 minutes, until golden brown. If colouring too quickly after 30 minutes of baking, cover them loosely with foil.

Transfer the loaves (and the parchment paper) to a wire rack and generously brush them with the melted butter. Gently roll the loaves in the icing sugar and sprinkle any remaining sugar over the top. Allow the stollen to cool completely, then wrap tightly in tinfoil.

It is 7:00 AM and the first loaves are already cooling on the racks my stepfather, Kevin, constructed for me. Baguettes and country loaves are clicking and cracking as they cool, the happy sound bakers refer to as the "singing of the loaves." My sisters, Katharina and Frances, make their way into the kitchen in search of breakfast. I offer them a loaf, still warm from the oven. Though tempted, they are more interested in the tray of pillowy cinnamon buns I baked the night before. "Save us a loaf," they mumble between mouthfuls of the sticky enriched dough. "We'll have it for lunch!"

Simplest Whole-Grain or Rye Bread 175
Vollkornbrot (Whole-Kernel Bread) 177
Whole-Grain Seed Loaf 181
Beer Bread (Inspired by Øllebrød) 183
The 33% Loaf 185
Oat & Honey Loaf 186

Rye & Whole-Grain Breads

In feudal times, white and refined flour was a status symbol for the wealthy, who favoured light and airy white breads and cakes. The heavier whole grains were left to the peasants or fed to the livestock. Whole wheat, barley, rye, and oats were baked into coarse loaves or cooked as porridge, no doubt in an attempt to soften the hard cereals and make them more palatable.

Today we have come full circle, advocating the health benefits of whole foods, fibre, and unrefined grains. Although white breads and carbohydrates are still the most popular, whole grains are slowly finding their way into mainstream foods and recipes. If you have been meaning to add more whole grains to your loaves, now is the time! These grains are a fantastic way to add additional flavour and texture (not to mention nutritional value) to your daily bread!

There is something reassuring about rye and whole-grain breads. They are sturdy, hearty, and heavy, not to mention jam-packed full of goodness. They promise to feed and nourish you and see you through long, harsh winters. These breads are decidedly underrated—a great pity in my opinion! If you are looking for breads that will keep you satiated and energized throughout the day, these loaves will make a happy addition to your lunchbox.

Rye breads are flavourful and sturdy and remain fresh for days. Some recipes even suggest letting the bread rest for two to three days (even a week) prior to slicing and eating! High in fibre and boasting a low glycemic index, rye bread is a good choice for diabetics or anyone interested in maintaining a healthy diet.

Rye falls within the wheat family but has a low glutenin content. This in turn leads to a lower gluten content in the dough and smaller, more compact loaves. People who suffer from gluten sensitivity or digestive issues may find it beneficial to favour rye bread over pure wheat breads. Note, however, that although rye is lower in gluten, it is definitely not gluten free. (See page 22 for more info on rye.)

The terms *wholemeal*, *whole grain*, and *whole wheat* are often used interchangeably; they simply refer to bread flours containing varying degrees of the entire wheat kernel, including the bran, germ, and endosperm. If you want to incorporate more whole grains into your diet, you can easily replace half of the white flour in a recipe with the same amount of whole-grain flour. Whole-grain flour boasts a slightly darker colour (think brownish/tan) and coarser texture because of the wheat bran. Unlike pure white wheat flour, baked goods made with whole-grain flours will be a little more dense, heavy, and compact. Because the bran is razor sharp, it easily severs the delicate gluten strands, which severely weakens the dough structure and inhibits the size of the final loaf. However, rest assured that, while you may be sacrificing volume, the final loaf is guaranteed to produce a tastier, more wholesome bread than a standard white loaf.

We now have a great variety of whole grains (unmilled berries) to choose from and have fun with. These cereals (when properly prepared through soaking, cooking, or sprouting) are an excellent way of adding even more flavour, texture, and goodness to your breads. Whole wheat, farro, spelt, barley, and rye are relatively easy to come by and are great pantry staples—wonderful in soups, salads, and even desserts. Heritage wheat varieties such as Red Fife, Kamut, Emmer, and Einkorn are not as readily available, though you may find them in natural-food stores or online.

Do not be put off by the extra step of having to soak the grains—your teeth are sure to thank you!

Simplest Whole-Grain or Rye Bread

This chapter is bursting with wholesome whole-grain recipes, but if you are looking to ease your way into this world, it couldn't be simpler! Choose any basic white bread recipe in this book and swap out 20 percent of the white flour for whole-wheat or rye flour. In other words, for a recipe calling for 500 g / 4 cups of white bread flour, you would use 100 g / 1 cup (20 percent) whole grain flour and 400 g / 3 cups (80 percent) white bread flour. Then proceed as per the instructions in the chosen recipe. (**NOTE:** A 50 percent whole grain or rye loaf works just as well, though you may need to add a little extra water to the dough.)

Another option is to add a portion of soaked whole grains (and/or seeds) to your go-to bread recipe. Simply soak 100 g of whole or crushed grains in 150 g of water (room temperature) and leave it to rest in a cool place overnight. The next day, drain off any water that has not been absorbed by the grains and set it aside. (I like to use the soaking water as part of the water content of the final dough to avoid wasting valuable nutrients or losing good flavours.) Add the soaked grains to the dough after the first hour of bulk fermentation and work them in with every hourly stretch and fold (much easier than trying to add in the grains prior to shaping the dough).

The above method can be applied to basic straight dough breads, pre-fermented breads, and sourdough loaves and should provide you with a great variety of breads.

Vollkornbrot (Whole-Kernel Bread)

This is a classic German loaf, though similar breads are found all over Europe. Some versions (like the Danish rugbrød) include molasses and dark ale, while others call for dark cocoa and brotgewürz (bread spice—a blend often including fennel, anise, caraway, and coriander). *Vollkornbrot* translates to "whole-kernel bread," which is an apt description, as it is loaded with a variety of whole, crushed, and coarsely milled grains. This hearty, robust, no-nonsense bread is usually made with whole-wheat, rye, or spelt flours and packed with whole-wheat kernels or rye berries and a generous mix of seeds.

MAKES 1 VERY LARGE OR 2 MEDIUM LOAVES

Day 1: Soaker

350 g / 2 cups mixed whole and crushed grains (spelt, rye, farro, barley, steel cut oats, and so on)
365 g / 2 ¾ cups mixed seeds (flax, sunflower, pumpkin, sesame)
700 g / 3 cups water

Combine the whole grains and seeds in a large bowl. Add the water and stir briefly. Cover and set aside in a cool place overnight.

Day 2: Dough

120 g ripe sourdough starter [24%]
500 g / 4 cups rye flour [100%]
15 g / 2 ½ tsp fine sea salt [3%]
8 g / 1 Tbsp bread spice (optional, see note) [1.6%]
400 g / 1 ½ cups water (including soaking water) or dark ale (room temperature) [80%]

Optional topping

Rolled oats or seeds

First thing in the morning on Day 2, feed your starter. To do this, you will dissolve 50 g starter in 50 g water and add 50 g of flour in a glass jar. Using a spatula or wooden spoon, stir the ingredients together until you have a smooth batter/paste. Make a mark on the jar indicating the level of the starter. Cover and set aside in a cozy place until doubled or tripled.

Once the starter is ready, measure out 120 g starter and reserve the remaining 30 g for future use. Drain the soaked seeds and grains in a sieve and save the soaking water if you want to add it to the dough as part of the overall hydration. (The soaking water will need to be weighed/measured so that you know how much additional water to add to the final dough.)

Mix the rye flour, salt, and bread spice (if using) together in a large bowl. Add the soaking water, additional water (or ale), and ripe starter to the dry ingredients. Work the mixture into a dough. Cover and set aside for 15–20 minutes.

Add the soaked mixture to the dough and massage it in. This will feel quite odd and messy, but do not lose heart! The mixture will now be rather dense and sticky, more like a thick, grainy clay, and unlike any bread dough you have encountered in my previous recipes. This is quite normal and no cause for concern. Cover the dough and set it aside in a warm spot for 3–4 hours of bulk fermentation until it starts to rise slightly and feels soft, spongy, and airy.

Grease a large Pullman pan (or two 8 ½-inch Pullman pans) with butter and sprinkle with seeds (optional). If you do not have a Pullman pan, see the note under Sourdough Sandwich Bread (page 147) to simulate the right baking conditions. Spoon the mixture into the prepared pan(s) and smooth the surface using a dough scraper or spatula. Sprinkle with rolled oats or seeds (optional) and cover with the lid(s) of the Pullman pan(s). Allow to rise for 50–60 minutes until somewhat risen and there are a few small holes dotted across the surface of the dough.

Preheat the oven to 450°F.

Bake for 30–35 minutes then remove the lid. Bake uncovered for 20–25 minutes. The loaf or loaves should pull away from the sides of the pan. If the loaf needs a little more time, switch off the oven and leave the bread to bask in the residual heat for 10–15 minutes.

Wrap the bread in a kitchen towel and cool on a wire rack overnight. Slice thinly to serve. This bread improves with age and will stay fresh for weeks if tightly wrapped in foil. It also freezes well.

Whole-Grain Seed Loaf

Vollkornbrot (see previous recipe) is a rather busy bread. Some would even say it's an acquired taste. Thus, I have toned it down a little in this recipe with a higher flour-to-seed-and-grain ratio than a traditional Vollkornbrot. You can play around with your choice of seeds, though I highly recommend using sunflower seeds! I have opted to use an equal mix of bread flour and dark rye flour. The result is a loaf that is a little more user-friendly and a lot more like bread—not to mention much easier to slice!

NOTE: This dough may require a little more liquid due to the high percentage of whole-grain flour. If necessary, add extra water or ale slowly and incrementally.

MAKES 1 LARGE OR 2 MEDIUM LOAVES

Day 1: Soaker

85 g / ½ cup mixed whole and crushed grains (spelt, rye, farro, steel cut oats, and so on)
50 g / ½ cup sunflower seeds
236 g / 1 cup water

Combine all the ingredients in a small bowl, cover, and allow to soak in a cool place overnight.

Day 2: Dough

250 g / 2 cups white bread flour [50%]
250 g / 2 cups dark rye flour (or spelt flour) [50%]
15 g / 2 ½ tsp fine sea salt [3%]
5 g / 1 ½ tsp instant yeast [1%] or 100g ripe sourdough starter [20%]
300–350 g / 1 ¼–1 ½ cups water or dark ale (room temperature) [60–70%]

Combine the flours, salt, yeast (or ripe sourdough), and water in a large bowl. (Resist adding additional water at this point.) Work into a basic dough, cover, and set aside for 1 hour.

Drain the soaked grains and seeds from Day 1. Add them to the dough and gently fold together. If the dough still seems dry, add a small amount of the soaking water and massage it in. Cover and set aside for an additional 1–2 hours, doing a stretch and fold after every hour (see page 40). If you used sourdough starter instead of yeast, the dough may require a total of 4–5 hours of fermentation before shaping.

Grease 1 13 × 4 × 4 or 2 8 ½-inch Pullman pans including the lid(s).

Shape the dough into a large oval and place in the prepared pan(s). Allow a final rising time of 60–80 minutes depending on how warm your kitchen is.

Preheat the oven to 450°F.

Bake for 50–60 minutes, removing the lid of the Pullman pan after the first 30 minutes. Continue baking until golden and baked through (it should pull away from the sides and sound hollow when knocked underneath).

Beer Bread (Inspired by Øllebrød)

Øllebrød is a rustic Danish breakfast porridge consisting of slices of dark rye bread and spices cooked in beer. Repurposing old bread into new dishes is a common practice all over Europe. The dry end pieces of rye breads are often soaked and added to new bread doughs or other baked goods, or used to brew alcoholic beverages such as kvass.

This recipe transforms the offcuts from a previous bake (or shop-bought loaf) into a fragrant, wholesome loaf of beer bread. So save a slice or two of dark rye and try your hand at this hearty loaf.

NOTES: The darker the beer you use, the stronger the malty flavour in the final loaf.

This loaf can also be made without the old-bread soaker: reduce the salt to 10 g (1 ¾ tsp) and use 375 g (1 ½ cups) beer.

MAKES 1 LARGE OR 2 SMALL LOAVES

Day 1: Old-bread soaker

100 g / ¾ cup old, dry, stale rye bread (the higher the rye content the better)

100 g / ½ cup water (room temperature)

If possible, break the old rye into smaller pieces and place in a bowl. Pour the water over the dry bread, cover, and allow to sit in a cool area overnight.

Day 2: Dough

400 g / 3 cups white bread flour [80%]

100 g / 1 cup dark rye or spelt flour [20%]

12 g / 2 tsp fine sea salt [2.4%]

5 g instant yeast [1%] or 100 g sourdough [20%]

340–360 g / 1 ½ cups beer [68–72%]

Mash the soaked bread from Day 1 as well as possible and set aside.

Combine the flours, salt, and instant yeast (if using) in a large bowl and mix briefly. If you are using the sourdough starter, add it to the bowl. Add the mashed bread mixture and 325 g / 1 ¼ cup of the beer and bring it together into a dough. Add more beer only if the dough is too firm or dry. If you used instant yeast, allow the dough to bulk ferment for 2–3 hours. For a dough made with sourdough starter, allow a minimum of 4 hours. Remember to perform a series of stretches and folds after every hour—except after the final hour of bulk fermentation.

Shape the dough into one large or two medium ovals and allow to proof seam side up in proofing baskets (bannetons) lightly dusted with flour. Allow the shaped loaves made with instant yeast to rise for an additional 40–60 minutes. For loaves made using sourdough, allow 1–2 hours.

Preheat the oven and the cast iron Dutch oven (if using) to 450°F.

Bake, covered, for 25–30 minutes. Remove the lid, and bake for an additional 15–20 minutes until golden. Allow to cool before slicing.

The 33% Loaf

This bread gets its name from each of the flours—white, whole-wheat, and dark rye flour—sitting at 33.33 percent. Nutritious, robust, and sturdy, this is a good winter bread, delicious with thick lashings of butter and also excellent with soup. It can be formed into a rustic artisan-style loaf and baked in a Dutch oven, a Pullman pan (for perfectly uniform slices), or two small (450 g / 1 lb) loaf pans. No need to add additional seeds or whole grains—this loaf is hearty enough.

MAKES 1 LARGE OR 2 SMALL LOAVES

167 g / 1 ½ cups white bread flour [33%]
167 g / 1 ¼ cups whole-wheat flour [33%]
167 g / 1 ¼ cups rye flour [33%]
12 g / 2 tsp fine sea salt [2.3%]
5 g / 1 heaped tsp instant yeast [1%] or 100 g / ½ cup sourdough starter [20%]
50 g / ¼ cup maple syrup or honey [10%]
390–400 g / 1 ¾ cup water (lukewarm) [78–80%]

If you want to use instant yeast to leaven the dough, follow the steps in the Rustic Country Loaf recipe (page 73). If you want to use sourdough, follow the steps in the Beginner's Sourdough recipe (page 133).

Oat & Honey Loaf

Few things are as satiating and comforting as oats. Unsurprisingly, this humble breakfast cereal has a long history of being mixed into bread doughs and other baked goods. They add a creamy texture and nutty flavour to the final loaf and are wonderfully nutritious too! In this recipe I have opted to mix the dough with warm milk, but you can use water with equally good results.

NOTE: This is a fantastic breakfast bread and perfect for school sandwiches.

MAKES 2 MEDIUM LOAVES

Day 1: Soaker

100 g / 1 cup rolled oats
190–200 g water (boiling)

Combine the oats and the boiling water in a small bowl, cover, and allow to soak overnight.

Day 2: Dough

450 g / 3 ⅝ cups white bread flour [90%]
50 g / 5 ½ Tbsp whole-wheat flour [10%]
13 g / 2 ¼ tsp fine sea salt [2.6%]
7 g / 1 heaped tsp instant yeast [1.4%] or 100g / ½ cup sourdough starter [20%]
375–400 g / 1 ½–1 ¾ cups milk or water (lukewarm) [75–80%]
50 g / 2 Tbsp honey or maple syrup [10%]

Optional topping

Rolled oats

If you want to use instant yeast to leaven the dough, follow the steps in the Rustic Country Loaf recipe (page 73). If you want to use sourdough, follow the steps in the Beginner's Sourdough recipe (page 133). Once mixed, cover and allow the dough to bulk ferment for 1 hour.

Return to the bowl and gently fold in the honey or maple syrup and the soaked oats from Day 1. Leave the dough to bulk ferment for an additional 2–3 hours. Perform a series of stretches and folds (page 40) after every hour. The stretches and folds will strengthen the dough (gluten) and will also ensure that the oats are properly distributed.

When the dough has undergone a bulk fermentation period of 3–4 hours and is well risen and puffy, it can be divided, shaped, and placed in the fridge overnight or allowed a final rise at room temperature. Tip the dough out onto a countertop lightly dusted with flour. Using a dough scraper, bench scraper, or sharp knife, divide the dough in half (a scale is useful if you want to be precise, but you can eye-ball the dough). Shape the dough into two round or oval loaves and place seam side up in bread baskets lightly dusted with flour. Alternatively, the dough can be placed in 2 small greased loaf pans (900 g / 2 lb). Cover and allow to rise. Loaves leavened with instant yeast can be left to rise at room temperature for 1 hour prior to being baked.

Sourdough loaves can be allowed 1–2 hours at room temperature, or until well risen and somewhat jiggly.

For best results, bake the loaves in a Dutch oven (see page 17) or Pullman pan. Bake the loaves as per the instructions in the Rustic Country Loaf recipe or the Beginner's Sourdough recipe. Uncovered sandwich loaves (no lids) must be baked with plenty of steam (see page 53). Preheat the oven as well as the Dutch oven (if cast iron), or the pan/skillet (to create steam). Enamel roasters, Pullman pans and loaf pans do not have to be preheated. Bake until beautifully golden and crusty. The loaves should sound hollow when tapped underneath. Allow to cool on a rack before serving.

Pita Pockets & Gyro Pita Wraps 191
Portuguese Rolls (Papo Secos) 195
Mosbolletjies (Grape Must Buns) 197
Dinner Rolls, Burger Buns & Hot Dog Rolls 198
BBQ Bread (Roosterkoek) 200

Rolls, Buns & Wraps

As impressive and reassuring as large loaves are, there is something to be said for smaller, individual, and hand-size breads. Buns, rolls, wraps, and scrolls are fantastic as quick meals. They conveniently require little to no slicing and due to their manageable size are unlikely to result in too much wastage. These are also excellent breads to keep in the freezer, as they can easily be defrosted when needed. Sweet, savoury, filled, or plain, these breads are a great addition to every baker's list of easy, everyday breads.

Pita Pockets & Gyro Pita Wraps

Thanks to the popularity of Greek gyros and Turkish doner kebabs, pita breads are finding their way onto many western shopping lists. Simple and wonderfully versatile, they can be used in much the same way we use wheat tortillas, naan breads, or even laffa. Any simple white bread dough will produce excellent pitas. You may use milk or yogurt instead of water and can play with the hydration too. Firmer (less-hydrated) doughs will yield the classic pita with the interior pocket, whereas higher-hydration doughs will yield gyro-style pitas, which are better suited as wraps or simple pizza bases.

NOTES: If you do not want the pitas to have bubbles or air pockets, you can dock (pierce) the dough with a dough docker or fork prior to baking.

The hydration (wetness) of the dough affects how easily you can roll out and shape the pitas. A higher hydration (70–75 percent) will be too sticky to roll out with a rolling pin. Instead, you will have to use a good amount of flour (on the countertop and the exterior of the dough) to shape (press) and stretch each piece out by hand. (The flour should not be worked into the dough, but instead used as a coating for easier handling of the wet dough.)

MAKES 4 LARGE OR 6 MEDIUM PITAS

1 batch Rustic Country Bread dough (page 87) at 60–65% hydration (300 or 325 g of water to 500 g of flour) or any yeasted white bread dough of your choice (including Government Loaf, sourdough, cold fermented, or pre-fermented)

Decide whether you want to make pita pockets or pita wraps, and reduce or increase the hydration in your chosen recipe accordingly. Follow the recipe instructions up to the end of bulk fermentation.

Divide the risen dough into 4 or 6 equal pieces and shape into round balls. Cover the dough and allow it to rest for 20–30 minutes.

Preheat the oven as well as a large baking sheet (or baking steel) to 450°F.

If you are making pita pockets, lightly dust the counter with flour and use a rolling pin to roll out each piece of dough into a flat disc approximately ¼ inch thick. Working quickly, place the discs roughly 1 inch apart on the pre-heated baking sheet(s). You can also bake 2 or 3 pitas at a time, if you find that easier. Bake for 1–2 minutes until the pitas balloon up, then flip them over and bake for an additional 1–2 minutes. Remove the pitas from the oven and wrap them in a clean kitchen towel until you are ready to serve them. Be careful not to overbake them, as they will dry out and crack.

If you are making gyro-style pitas, dust the counter and the dough ball with flour. Flatten and stretch each dough ball with your hands until it is roughly 8 inches in diameter. Bake on a preheated baking sheet/steel for 6–8 minutes. They will bubble up in some spots but will not create a perfect pocket. Allow the pitas to develop a few patches of colour before removing them from the oven and placing them inside a clean kitchen towel on top of a cooling rack.

While baking the pitas in the oven is faster for large batches, they can also be cooked on the stovetop. This method gives the pitas more colour and character. Heat a frying pan over medium heat. Cook each pita for approximately 30 seconds and flip it over as soon as it starts to bubble. Cook for an additional 30–40 seconds then flip over again. Cook the pita pocket until it balloons up completely or the gyro pita until it has developed a few patches of colour. Transfer to a clean dish towel on top of a cooling rack and wrap the pitas in the towel so that they remain soft.

Portuguese Rolls (Papo Secos)

The humble Portuguese roll is a fantastic everyday roll. Not too flimsy, and with a crispy exterior, they are perfect for mopping up the delectable juices of beef trinchado (a spicy Portuguese stew) and are the proud vessels of the classic prego roll, a well-buttered sandwich filled with perfectly grilled steak or chicken and drenched in garlic and peri-peri sauce. While any basic white bread dough can be used to make Portuguese-style rolls, you may need to reduce the hydration a little to ensure easier shaping and handling of the dough.

NOTE: For this recipe I recommend a hydration of around 58–65% (290–325 g water to 500 g flour).

MAKES 6–9 ROLLS

1 batch Government Loaf dough (page 67) or 1 batch Rustic Country Bread dough (page 87)

Prepare the dough as per the instructions in the chosen recipe and reduce the hydration if applicable (recommended). Once the dough has completed the bulk fermentation period, you are ready to shape the Portuguese rolls.

Line a baking sheet with parchment paper and lightly dust with flour.

Divide the risen dough into 6–9 equal pieces (or the number and size of your choice). Shape each piece of dough into a round and place it on the prepared baking sheet. Cover and allow to rest for 15–20 minutes.

Flatten each dough ball into a disc of approximately 5–6 inches. Use the side of your hand to make a deep line in the centre of the disc. Gently pull/tug the dough at each end of the line you have created, stretching it into a rough oval. Fold the dough in half (along the centre dividing line) and pinch the ends on either side to seal them off. Place the buns seam-side down to proof in the folds of a couche (proofing cloth or large kitchen towel, see page 48) for 45–60 minutes until doubled.

Preheat the oven to 420°F.

Place the buns seam-side up (1 inch apart) on the prepared baking sheet. Bake for 15–20 minutes, or until lightly golden brown. Tap the rolls on the bottom to check for doneness, they should sound hollow. If in doubt, bake 5 minutes longer. Allow to cool before serving.

Mosbolletjies (Grape Must Buns)

These buns are closely associated with the Cape Winelands in South Africa. Traditionally leavened with mos (grape must) and spiced with aniseed, mosbolletjies were introduced to South Africa by the French Huguenots in the late 1600s. Because grape must is no longer a common ingredient, modern mosbolletjies are often made with fermented raisin water or white grape juice and yeast. These small balls of enriched dough are tightly packed in a loaf pan yielding soft pull-apart rolls that are a real treat enjoyed warm with plenty of butter.

MAKES 12 SMALL MOSBOLLETJIES

Dough

500 g / 4 cups bread or all-purpose flour [100%]
35 g / ¼ cup sugar [7%]
10 g / 1 ¾ tsp salt [2%]
10 g / 3 tsp instant yeast [2%]
4–5 g / 2 tsp aniseed [0.8–1%]
130–145 g / ½ cup white grape juice (room temperature) or fermented raisin water [26–29%]
50 g / ¼ cup butter (melted) [10%]
130–145 g / ½ cup whole milk (lukewarm) [26–29%]

Topping

15 mL / 1 Tbsp warm milk or melted honey

Combine all the dry ingredients in a large bowl. Add the grape juice and butter to the bowl and gently start mixing. Slowly add the lukewarm milk and work into a basic dough. Knead the dough on the countertop until smooth and elastic (no need to use any additional flour unless the dough remains sticky after 5–10 minutes of kneading). Form the dough into a ball and return it to the mixing bowl. Cover and allow it to rise in a cozy place for 2–3 hours.

Grease a large loaf pan or 2 small pans.

Remove the risen dough from the bowl and knead briefly. Portion it into 12 equal pieces and shape them into balls. Tightly pack the balls of dough into the prepared pan(s). Loosely cover them with a damp tea towel and allow to rise for 45–60 minutes.

Preheat the oven to 355°F.

Bake for 30–40 minutes, until golden brown. Allow to cool slightly before turning the buns out onto a wire rack. Brush with warm milk or melted honey to give the bread extra shine.

Enjoy the warm mosbolletjies with butter and tea or a good cup of boeretroos (coffee, literally “farmer’s comfort” in Afrikaans). To make mosbeskuit (rusks), gently break the bread into pieces and dry them out in a cool oven (200°F) overnight, or until dry.

Dinner Rolls, Burger Buns & Hot Dog Rolls

Whether you attend a formal dinner, family BBQ, or simple picnic, buns and rolls are bound to feature in some shape or form! Great as a starter or side (think dinner rolls and sliders) or as part of the main meal, the humble bun can easily be reinvented to suit many a culinary need. Small, large, pull-apart or individual—the details are up to you, so have some fun and get creative while you are at it!

1 batch of dough from the Government Loaf (page 67), Kitke (page 155), or Milk Bread (page 157)

Prepare the dough as per your chosen recipe and allow the dough to rise until the dough is ready for shaping.

Line one or more baking sheets (depending on what you have available at home) with parchment paper.

After the final hour of bulk fermentation lightly dust the counter with flour. Divide the dough into 16, 12, 9, or 6 equal pieces. Shape each piece of dough into a tight round. For pull-apart buns place the shaped rolls on the prepared baking sheet(s), spaced about ½ an inch apart so the rolls can rise and expand into each other. Cover and allow to rise for 60–80 minutes.

Preheat the oven to 380°F. (The same temperature is used for all the bun shapes.)

Bake for 25–30 minutes, until golden brown. (If the rolls are browning too quickly, carefully lay a sheet of tinfoil over top.)

Remove from the oven and immediately brush with melted butter. Allow the rolls to cool on the tray for at least 10 minutes before turning out on a wire rack.

For individual dinner rolls: Bake for 15–20 minutes, or until golden. Brush with melted butter (optional).

For hot dog rolls: Divide the dough into 8 equal pieces (approximately 100 g each). Shape each piece into a log approximately 6 inches long. Cover and allow to rise for 60–80 minutes. Bake for 15–20 minutes, or until golden.

For burger buns: Leave enough space between the shaped rolls so they do not rise into each other (approximately 1 ½ inches). Lightly flatten the risen rolls with the palm of your hand then brush with egg wash (1 egg + 15 g / 1 Tbsp water whisked together) and sprinkle with sesame seeds. Cover and allow to rise for 60–80 minutes. Bake for 15–20 minutes, or until golden.

BBQ Bread (Roosterkoek)

Rooster is the Afrikaans word for grill and *koek* translates to cake, but these should not be confused with Welsh griddle cakes! Roosterkoek will make a great addition to your campside menu, though they require a little skill and patience. Rush the dough and the bread will be dense and stodgy. Rush the fire and the bread will be charred but raw. Serve with lots of butter as a side to grilled meat or snoek (a salty, often smoked fish common in the Southern Hemisphere). Roosterkoek is distinguished by the somewhat blackened grill lines on the exterior of the bread.

MAKES 6 LARGE ROOSTERKOEKE

1 batch Rustic Country Loaf dough (page 73) at 60% hydration (300 g / 1 ¼ cup water to 500 g / 4 cups flour) or 1 batch Government Loaf dough (page 67)

Prepare the dough as per the chosen recipe (reducing the hydration if using the Rustic Country Loaf dough). Allow the dough to rise for a minimum of 2 hours prior to shaping. It is a good idea to factor the rising time into your fire or grill schedule. The fire will need to die down before the buns can be baked, whereas the BBQ can be turned on at short notice.

On a lightly floured surface, flatten the dough out into a rectangle (approximately 8 × 12 inches). To do this, you can use a rolling pin or your hands. Use a bench scraper or sharp knife to divide the dough into 6 equal pieces. The roosterkoeke can be left as squares or shaped into rounds. Separate the pieces slightly (1 ½ inches) so they don't rise into each other, then cover and allow to rise for 30–40 minutes.

Lightly flour each roosterkoek then place them on the grill over warm/gentle coals. Grill for 10 minutes then flip the buns over and grill for an additional 5–10 minutes. The roosterkoeke should show a bit of colour and a good couple of grill lines. Tap the bottoms for doneness (they should sound hollow). If in doubt, return to the fire/BBQ and bake a little longer.

Immediately enjoy a hot, smoky roosterkoek with plenty of butter!

It is lunchtime on a Friday and Maboneng is dizzyingly busy, though nothing compared to the happy chaos that ensues on Saturdays and Sundays, when tourists and locals alike descend on Fox Street and surrounds.

Mr. Washington and Mama Clementina are slicing the last of the day's baguettes. Filled with generous quantities of ham, salami, or pastrami in addition to slices of cheddar cheese, gherkins, lettuce, and tomato, the Gourmet Sandwiches disappear from the display case faster than they can be made. And just like that, we are sold out and done for the day.

Ravenous after a gruelling morning of baking, I venture out through the large Urban Fox doors in search of sustenance. As I walk, I smell the tantalizing aroma of grilling meat wafting out from Sha'p Braai and the scent of spicy shakshuka being prepared at Eat Your Heart Out. The informal vendors are peddling their wares while buskers add rhythm to the sea of noise.

I find Kassa sitting outside his restaurant, Little Addis, enjoying an Ethiopian coffee. "The usual?" he asks, smiling. I nod with a grin. The vegetarian mixed portion, served with teff injera, is a particular favourite. As I wait for the food, we catch up on the latest community news, frequently interrupted by friendly and familiar faces.

Montreal Bagels 205
Laugenbrotchen (German Pretzel Buns) 207
Dombolo (Traditional African Steamed Bread) 210
Vetkoek (Fried Bread) 211
Fried Dough Variations 212
Dad's Pancakes (Pannekoek) 215

Boiled, Fried & Steamed Breads

There are many ways to make *and* bake bread! Some breads are baked in the ashes of a fire, some are steamed, others are fried, and yet others are boiled prior to being baked. Each technique lends a unique flavour or texture to the resulting bread. Bagels and pretzels would not be as gloriously chewy if they were not boiled prior to facing the heat of the oven. And the softest, airiest, most indulgent of doughnuts can only be achieved by deep frying.

Montreal Bagels

Introduced to Canada in the early twentieth century by Polish Jewish immigrants, Montreal bagels are vastly different from their New York cousins. The Canadian bagels are sweeter, more chewy, and boast a larger hole. Montreal bagels are also rolled by hand and baked in traditional wood-fired ovens, in contrast to the commercially manufactured NYC bagel. And where the American bagels are made from a lean dough, Canadian bagels are enriched with eggs, oil, and plenty of honey. Curiously though, traditional Montreal bagels are made without the addition of salt.

NOTE: For authentic and extra chewy bagels, it is recommended to use high protein bread flour. Although conventional bread or AP flour will also produce a decent bagel, extending the poaching time by a few minutes will help achieve the characteristic chewiness.

INGREDIENTS NOTE: Diastatic malt powder is made from grain (wheat or barley) that has been sprouted, dried, and ground into a fine powder. This powder contains active enzymes which help transform starches into sugar and assist with the rising process. Thus it is a natural dough enhancer.

Everything bagel seasoning is a popular seasoning (mix) consisting of black and white sesame seeds, poppy seeds, dried onion and garlic, as well as salt flakes.

MAKES 8–9 BAGELS

Sponge

100 g / ¾ cup bread flour [20%]
12 g / 3 ½ tsp instant yeast [2.4%]
100 g / ½ cup water [20%]

Dough

400 g / 3 ¼ cups high protein bread flour [14%], normal bread flour, or AP flour [80%]
12 g / 2 tsp fine sea salt [2.4%] (optional but not traditional)
5 g / ⅝ Tbsp diastatic malt powder [1%] (see note)
45 g / ¼ cup oil [9%]
2 eggs (beaten)
50 g / 3 Tbsp + 1 tsp water (lukewarm) [10%]
130 g / ½ cup honey [26%]

Honey bath

90 g / ¼ cup honey
3 L / 2.6 quarts water

Topping

Sesame seeds, poppy seeds, or everything bagel seasoning (see note)

Montreal bagel enthusiasts typically enjoy their bagels with cream cheese and lox (a fillet of brined salmon). And up until recently, the iconic Liberté cream cheese reigned supreme. The original brand was founded in Quebec in 1936 by Jewish immigrants from Eastern Europe. As a top-quality dairy product with a unique flavour and texture, this cream cheese paired beautifully with the Montreal bagel and soon became an integral part of the Montreal food scene. But in 2022, Montrealers were devastated to learn that production of their beloved spreadable cheese had ceased.

For the sponge (pre-ferment), combine the ingredients and mix well. Cover and set aside for 15 minutes (or until bubbly and frothy).

For the dough, combine the dry ingredients in a large bowl. Add the oil, eggs, water, honey, and sponge mixture. Combine all the ingredients and mix into a basic dough. (Fold, knead, squeeze the mixture until a rough and sticky mass is achieved.) Transfer the dough to a lightly floured countertop and knead for a few minutes, until smooth. Return the dough to the bowl, cover, and set aside for 1 hour.

Gently deflate the dough then knead again briefly. Cover and set aside for an additional 1–2 hours. You can also let it rise in the fridge overnight, but it will have to sit at room temperature for 1–2 hours before continuing with the next step.

For the honey bath, combine the water and honey in a large pot and put it on to boil.

Divide the dough into 8 or 9 equal pieces. One by one, roll each piece of dough into a 10-inch log. Loop the dough around your hand so that the 2 end pieces overlap within the palm of your hand. To seal the end pieces together, gently but firmly press down onto the dough and roll the dough under the palm of your hand (similar movement to rolling out a baguette). Once the ends are joined together, set the shaped bagel aside and repeat with the remaining dough.

Preheat the oven to 450°F. Line a baking sheet with parchment paper.

Boil the bagels 3 at a time for a minute on each side (or 2 minutes per side for extra chewy bagels). With a slotted spoon, transfer the boiled bagels to a cooling rack to drain.

Moving quickly, roll the still warm bagels in the topping/seasoning of your choice until they are well coated, then arrange on the prepared baking sheet.

Bake in the preheated oven for 16–18 minutes, or until golden and crusty. (When baking in the traditional wood-fired ovens, bagels are flipped over at the halftime mark. You can choose to do this too, which will give you a more even outer crust.) Transfer to a wire rack to cool.

Laugenbrötchen (German Pretzel Buns)

Pretzel dough is traditionally enriched with schmalz (animal fat or lard) and contains a small percentage of malt powder. The firm dough makes it easy to form into a variety of shapes and ensures that the dough will retain its shape (and not collapse) when boiled. While the traditional pretzel shape is fun to make once in a while, I prefer making laugenstangen (oblong buns) or laugenbrötchen (round buns), as these are more practical and fantastic for sandwiches! *Lauge* refers to the lye (or alkaline solution) in which these breads are boiled prior to being baked. This recipe avoids the caustic and cumbersome nature of lye and uses a baking soda bath instead.

BAKING NOTE: German pretzels have a darker and crispier crust than American soft pretzels. Bake the pretzels according to your own taste and preference.

SERVING NOTE: Pretzel buns are delicious on their own, but they also make a fantastic addition to a German-themed harvest board. Think cured meats, strong cheeses, gherkins (pickles), sauerkraut, German mustard, and a few pints of weißbier to wash it down. Guten appetit!

MAKES 6 LARGE OR 9 SMALL BUNS

Dough

500 g / 4 cups white bread or all-purpose flour [100%]
4 g / 1 ¼ tsp instant yeast [0.8%]
5 g / ⅝ Tbsp diastatic malt powder [1%] (see note on page 205)
10 g / 2 tsp fine sea salt [2%]
40 g / ⅛ cup schmalz / butter / lard / oil [8%]
280–300 g / 1 cup water (lukewarm) [56–60%]

Soda bath

2.5 L / 10 ½ cups water
150 g / ⅔ cup baking soda

Optional toppings

Pretzel salt, salt flakes, or pearl salt

Combine all the dry ingredients in a large bowl. Add the schmalz, butter, or oil to the bowl and gently massage it into the flour with your hands. Add the water and continue working the mixture with your hands until it comes together into a dough. Transfer to a lightly floured work surface and knead until smooth (5–10 minutes). Return the dough to the bowl, cover, and set aside for 1 hour.

Gently deflate the dough and knead it again briefly. Cover and allow the dough to rest for an additional hour. You can also allow it to rest in the fridge overnight, but be sure to give it 2–3 hours at room temperature before shaping it the next day.

Divide the dough into 6 or 9 equal pieces and pre-shape into rounds. Cover and allow to rest for 5–10 minutes before shaping each piece into an oblong log, round bun or classic pretzel shape. For oblong buns, flatten the dough ball into a disc and roll it up into a tight scroll before sealing it and rolling briefly under the palm of your hand (similar to shaping a demi baguette). Repeat with the remaining dough

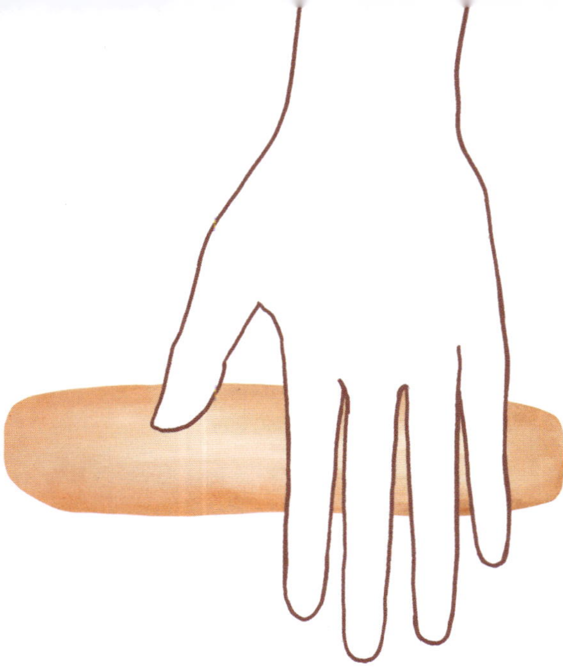

pieces. For round buns, shape the dough pieces into tight rounds then gently flatten each piece with the palm of your hand.

Cover and allow the dough to rise for 60 minutes at room temperature.

Preheat the oven to 425°F. Line a baking sheet with parchment paper.

For the soda bath, bring the water to a boil in a large pot and add the baking soda. Reduce to a simmer and gently transfer the buns into the baking soda solution (3 or 4 at a time). Allow to simmer for ½ minute on each side, then remove with a skimmer or slotted spoon and place on a cooling rack and allow the excess moisture to drip off the rolls.

Transfer the buns to the prepared baking sheet. Sprinkle with salt (if using), then score (slice) a cross into the surface of the dough (about ¼ inch deep) with a baker's lame or sharp knife. Bake for 20–25 minutes, until the crust turns a deep, reddish brown and the buns sound hollow when tapped underneath.

Dombolo (Traditional African Steamed Bread)

This bread is a staple food in South Africa. Dombolo can be baked as loaves or made into individual dumplings. The risen dough is steamed in a heat-proof container inside a pot of simmering water. Dombolo is usually served with a hearty meat stew or the spicy South African vegetable relish called *chakalaka*. The dumplings can also be cooked directly on top of the stew instead of in a separate vessel. Whenever there was extra dough left over at the bakery, Mama Clementina, a Sotho lady who worked with us, would turn it into dombolo.

NOTE: You may opt to make a full batch of dough and use half of it for the dombolo and the other half for Portuguese Rolls (page 195) or Vetkoek (page 211).

MAKES 1 MEDIUM OR 6–8 INDIVIDUAL DOMBOLO

½ batch Government Loaf dough (page 67)
Butter (for greasing heat-proof vessel or ramekins)

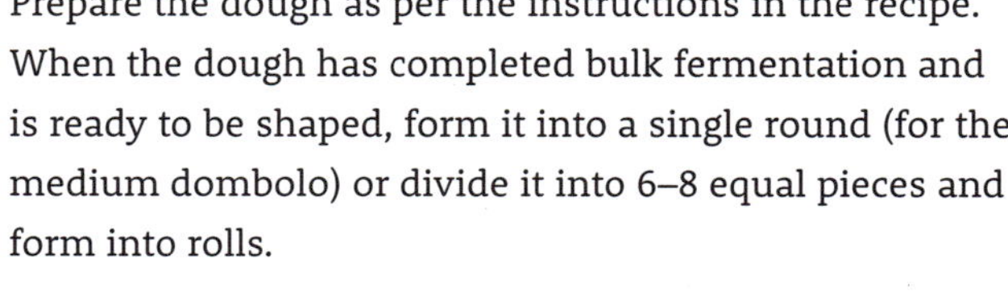

Prepare the dough as per the instructions in the recipe. When the dough has completed bulk fermentation and is ready to be shaped, form it into a single round (for the medium dombolo) or divide it into 6–8 equal pieces and form into rolls.

If you are steaming in a separate pot, grease a single heat-proof container (an enamel pot/bowl will work well) or 6–8 ramekins and place the dough in them. If you are steaming the dough on top of a stew, place it on a baking sheet to rise. For all three options, allow the dough to rise for approximately 40 minutes.

When steaming the dombolo in ramekins or a single heat-proof vessel inside a pot of hot water, the vessel(s) should be about ⅓ immersed. Place the lid securely on the pot and allow it to simmer gently. Steam the individual dombolo for about 15–20 minutes and the larger dombolo for about 30–45 minutes. When cooking the dombolo dumplings on top of a stew, lightly dust the buns with flour and very gently place the risen ball(s) of dough in the pot during the last 15–20 minutes of cooking time. Large dombolo should be sliced before serving.

dombolo (dumpling)

sliced dombolo

Vetkoek (Fried Bread)

There are countless takes on fried dough around the world. Spanish churros, Greek loukoumades, Turkish lokma, French beignets, Italian zeppole (and bomboloni), and Canadian beaver tails are just a few examples of international fried-dough delights.

The South African fried dough equivalent is similar to the Dutch oliebollen and offers two distinct variations, vetkoek and magwinya. Vetkoek are large, deep-fried buns traditionally stuffed with curried mince or cheese. Magwinya are smaller and considerably sweeter, often sold by informal food vendors or at local convenience stores called spaza shops.

MAKES 6 VETKOEKE (OR 12 MAGWINYA)

1 batch Government Loaf dough (page 67) or Kitke dough (page 155)
Sunflower oil (or vegetable oil) for frying

Prepare the dough as per the chosen recipe and let it rise twice.

Once the dough is ready to be shaped, divide it into 6 equal pieces. On a lightly floured surface, shape each piece into a flat disc about ¾-inch thick—you can use your hands or a rolling pin. Cover and allow to rest for 30–60 minutes. (Do not skip this final rest, or you risk dense, heavy, stodgy vetkoeke.)

Pour sunflower oil into a deep frying pan or saucepan and heat to about 330°F. To check whether the oil is hot enough, place a small piece of dough in the pan. When the oil starts to bubble around the piece of dough, you are ready to fry your vetkoeke.

Fry 2–3 vetkoeke (or however many you can comfortably fit into the pan) in the hot oil until golden brown underneath, then carefully flip over. Continue frying until both sides are equally golden and it sounds hollow when you tap on it. Transfer to a wire rack lined with paper towels (to absorb any excess oil). Allow to cool for 5–10 minutes.

Cut open the side and fill with curried mince or a filling of your choice. For a fantastic twist on the classic Sloppy Joe, simply swap the burger buns for warm vetkoeke—you can thank me later!

Fried Dough Variations

Both the Kitke dough and its variations (page 155) and the Milk Bread dough (page 157) can be used to make beautifully soft, airy, delicious doughnuts. Think Berliner (German jam doughnuts) or beaver tails (Canadian doughnuts). And don't be afraid of adding a little lemon or orange zest to the dough for extra flavour!

BERLINER

1 batch enriched dough of your choice
Sunflower oil (for frying)
165 g / ½ cup strawberry/ raspberry/ plum jam or vanilla custard (for filling) or filling of your choice
Caster sugar and/or confectioner's sugar (for dusting)

Line a baking sheet with parchment paper.

Once the dough has risen for 2–3 hours, divide it into 9–12 equal pieces. Shape the pieces into rounds and place them on the prepared baking sheet. Gently press down on each bun with the palm of your hand to flatten them slightly. (NOTE: If you choose not to flatten the dough, the resulting doughnuts will be spherical). Cover and allow to rise for 1 hour.

Add oil to a deep frying pan or saucepan and heat to about 330°F. If you don't have a thermometer, you can test the oil by adding a small piece of dough to the pot. When the oil starts to bubble around the dough, you are ready to fry your Berliner.

Use a slotted spoon to transfer the risen dough into the hot oil. Do not overcrowd the doughnuts—rather fry them in batches of 3–4. Fry for 1–2 minutes on each side. Again using the slotted spoon, remove from the oil, place on a rack lined with a few sheets of paper towel, and allow to cool for 5–10 minutes.

Roll each Berliner in caster sugar (a soup bowl or dinner plate will work well). Then allow the doughnuts to cool completely before filling them. You will need a piping bag with a long nozzle to fill each doughnut with the jam, jelly, or custard of your choice. To do this, push the tip of the nozzle right into the centre and squeeze in the jam until you start to feel resistance. Repeat with the remaining doughnuts. Lightly dust with icing sugar before serving (optional).

BEAVER TAILS

1 batch enriched dough of your choice
Sunflower or vegetable oil for frying
Cinnamon sugar for coating/dusting

Divide the dough into 12 equal pieces and loosely shape them into rounds. Use a rolling pin to roll out each piece of dough. (Cover the pieces you're not working on with a clean kitchen towel to prevent them from drying out.) The idea is to stretch and elongate the dough so it resembles a beaver's tail (a flat oval roughly ¼ inch thick). Cover and allow to rise for 20–30 minutes.

Add oil to a deep frying pan or saucepan and heat to about 330°F. If you don't have a thermometer, you can test the oil by adding a small piece of dough to the pot. When the oil starts to bubble around the dough, you are ready to fry your Beaver Tails.

Carefully place a piece of dough into the hot oil. Do not overcrowd the Beaver Tails, rather fry them 1 at a time or in batches of 2 (if your saucepan is large enough). Fry for 1–2 minutes on each side until golden brown and puffy. Use tongs to flip them over as well as when removing them from the hot oil. Place on a rack lined with a few sheets of paper towel, and allow to cool for 5–10 minutes then generously coat each Beaver Tail with cinnamon sugar.

Dad's Pancakes (Pannekoek)

When the first drops of rain hit the dry, dusty soil and a familiar sweetness fills the air, I am immediately transported back to my childhood. Rainy days are pancake days. When we were little, even a cloudy, overcast day was enough to send us running to the kitchen, announcing (rather earnestly) that pancakes were in order. So, out came the frying pan, and within minutes a fresh stack of pannekoek, and sometimes plaatkoekies (flapjacks), would be served for breakfast, lunch, or afternoon tea. We devoured them by the dozens!

FREEZER NOTE: These pancakes also freeze very well.

MAKES 6 OR 7 PANCAKES

490 g / 2 cups milk
2 eggs
21 g / 1 ½ Tbsp butter (melted, optional)
3 g / ½ tsp salt
125 g / 1 cup all-purpose or cake flour
Sunflower oil or butter for frying

Optional toppings

Cinnamon
Sugar
Lemon juice
Steamed apples with cinnamon
Nutella

Combine the milk, eggs, melted butter (if using), and salt in a medium bowl and whisk together. Slowly start adding the flour, whisking after every addition. Continue until all the flour has been incorporated and you have a thin but silky batter. Cover and allow to rest in the fridge (or a cool place) for 30 minutes.

Heat a heavy-based frying pan or crêpe pan on medium heat and spread a little oil or butter across the surface, just enough to coat the pan (drain off any excess).

To test whether the oil/butter is hot enough, allow a small drop of batter to drip into the pan. Once small bubbles start to form around the batter, you are ready to fry your pancakes.

Use a ladle or measuring cup to add a little batter to the pan, about half a cup per pancake. (If using a smaller pan, you will use less of the batter to coat the pan. While a smaller pan will produce smaller pancakes, you will have a higher yield—more pancakes!) Carefully tilt and swirl the pan to evenly distribute a thin layer of batter across the entire base of the pan. Depending on the size of your pan, you may need to use a little more or a little less batter. It takes a little practice, but you will improve with every pancake. Don't be disheartened if the first pancake flops or tears (this happens often!). It will still be delicious with a good dusting of cinnamon sugar.

Fry the pancake until small bubbles become visible on the surface of the pancake and the batter no longer looks wet. Gently loosen the sides of the pancake with a spatula and carefully lift the edge to assess its colour. When the pancake is golden or has brown spots, flip it over and continue to bake for another 1–2 minutes, or until both sides boast a caramel hue. Remove from the pan and place on a dinner plate, with a second plate over top to keep them warm. Continue with the remaining batter until all the pancakes are cooked, stacking them on top of each other.

Serve the stack of warm pancakes with cinnamon sugar (see cinnamon sugar mixture on page 164 minus the butter) and lemon juice. (Although the lemon juice is optional, the tartness adds a wonderful contrast and freshness to the sweet and fragrant cinnamon sugar.) Alternatively, start with savoury fillings (think bacon and aged cheddar or spinach and feta) then move on to the sweet fillings for dessert. Steamed apples with cinnamon also make a delicious filling, as does vanilla ice cream with golden syrup. Sweet or savoury, I recommend doubling or even tripling the recipe, as these disappear in the blink of an eye!

It is early May 2020 and the Covid-19 lockdown is wreaking havoc on local businesses, especially the small businesses! I hug the certificate declaring the bakery an "essential service" as we drive past the police roadblock into downtown Johannesburg, where the bakery is situated.

Wearing our masks, we mix, shape, and bake the day's orders. We work in silence, the mood dampened by the uncertainty and seriousness of the time.

Today is our first day delivering directly to our customers' homes. We have had to change our business model overnight. We are blown away by the incredible support. Within weeks we employed two drivers to share the load with us. Special times!

Cornbread (Mieliebrood) 221

Scones 222

Wholemeal Soda Bread 223

Mandy's Savoury Cheese & Herb Bread 225

Vegan Banana Bread 227

Quick Breads

Not all breads are leavened with yeast. We've all been there, when life gets busy and there is no time to wait for yeast to work its magic. In such instances, chemical leavening agents such as baking powder and bicarbonate of soda will help you produce a deliciously wholesome loaf in a fraction of the time it would take a yeasted dough to properly develop. Quick breads are more compact and cake-like than their yeast-leavened cousins, but they provide a hearty and satisfying solution when you have to put food on the table in a hurry. As an added bonus, quick breads are not as susceptible to changing weather or climate conditions as yeast leavened breads, making them more reliable and consistent—provided, of course, that you measure your ingredients accurately . . .

Cornbread (Mieliebrood)

Originally grown by indigenous people in the Americas, corn became a popular commodity amongst seafarers and international traders and thus found its way to some of the farthest corners of the world. Corn was first introduced to Africa by Portuguese merchants. In South Africa, mielie meal (coarse corn flour) quickly became a staple food due to its affordability and shelf-stable nature. It is traditionally eaten in the form of pap (porridge) or phuthu (a rustic porridge of varying consistency), though hot and buttery cornbread is hugely popular at BBQS.

NOTE: This recipe produces one small loaf, but it can easily be doubled and baked in a large Pullman pan when catering for a big group. Optional extras include chilies, cheese, herbs, or spring onions.

MAKES 1 SMALL LOAF

140 g / 1 cup all-purpose or bread or cake flour
160 g / 1 cup maize meal (alternatively, coarse cornmeal or polenta)
50 g / ¼ cup sugar
15 g / 3 tsp baking powder
6 g / 1 tsp salt
2–3 eggs (beaten)
240 g / 1 cup buttermilk or Greek yogurt or amasi (a fermented milk product similar to yogurt)
50 g / ¼ cup butter (melted) or olive oil
175 g / 1 cup fresh or frozen corn kernels (chopped)

Preheat the oven to 390°F. Grease the sides of a small (900 g / 2 pound) loaf pan and line it with parchment paper.

Combine all the dry ingredients in a medium bowl and stir together briefly. Add the milk, melted butter (or oil), eggs, and corn to the dry ingredients. Fold into a smooth mixture, until no dry flour is visible.

Transfer the batter to the prepared pan. Bake in the preheated oven for 45 minutes, or until a skewer (or toothpick) inserted into the centre comes out clean. Serve warm with plenty of butter.

Scones

South African cuisine draws inspiration from a great variety of foods from many culinary traditions. It is a melting pot of flavours—think African, Malay, Indian, British, French, Dutch, German, Greek, Italian, and Portuguese, to name only a few! One of the more popular English contributions is the classic scone. These soft, crumbly delights have universal appeal and make for a special breakfast or afternoon treat served with butter, cheese, and jam. A close cousin of the humble bannock, scones are one of the earliest forms of quick bread.

NOTE: The amount of liquid you need may vary from one brand of flour to the next.

FREEZER NOTE: Scones are another great item to add to the freezer, ready to be warmed up at short notice. A sure crowd pleaser!

MAKES 10–20 SCONES

500 g / 2 cups all-purpose or cake flour
25 g / 2 Tbsp sugar
30–35 g / 2 Tbsp baking powder
5 g / ¾ tsp salt
140 g / ½ cup butter (grated or cubed)
2 eggs (beaten)
130–150 g / ½ cup milk, cream, buttermilk, or Greek yogurt

Egg wash

1 egg (beaten)

Combine all the dry ingredients in a medium bowl. Add the butter and gently work it into the flour using your hands. The mixture should resemble soft breadcrumbs. Add the eggs and half of the milk and gently fold in. Add a little more milk and continue mixing until the mixture just comes together, not dry or floury and not overly wet or sticky. (You may not need all the milk, so be sure to read the dough.) Lightly compact the mixture between your hands, shaping it into a ball or basic square, but do not overwork the dough. Cover and refrigerate for 20–30 minutes.

Dust the countertop with flour and lightly roll out the dough to about ¾–1 inch thick. Using a round scone or cookie cutter, cut out discs of dough. (A well-floured drinking glass or mug will do the trick too.) Alternatively you may choose to simply use a bench scraper or sharp knife to cut the dough into square pieces.

Preheat the oven to 355°F. Line a baking sheet with parchment paper.

Place the scones onto the prepared baking sheet, leaving some space between them. Brush the top of the scones with the egg wash. Bake them in the preheated oven for 15–20 minutes, or until golden brown.

Serve warm with butter and jam or whipped cream and jam for an extra-special treat!

Wholemeal Soda Bread

If you have paged through older recipe books, you will undoubtedly have come across some version of this simple wholemeal or whole-wheat loaf. Baking soda (bicarbonate of soda) and yogurt (or buttermilk) work together to produce a bread that is hearty, healthy, and satisfying. You can easily add seeds, nuts, or raisins, though a plain loaf enjoyed with butter won't disappoint either!

MAKES 1 LOAF

Butter (for greasing pan)
500 g / 4 cups wholemeal or whole-wheat flour
8 g / 1 ¼ tsp salt
7 g / 1 ½ tsp bicarbonate of soda
13 g / 1 Tbsp sugar (optional)
500 g / 2 cups plain yogurt, buttermilk, kefir, or amasi (a fermented milk product similar to yogurt)
14 g / 1 Tbsp sunflower oil

Preheat the oven to 355°F. Grease a large loaf pan with butter.

Combine all the dry ingredients in a large bowl and stir briefly. Add the yogurt (or dairy alternative) and oil and fold together until no dry flour is visible. The mixture should be quite moist. If overly dry, add a little water or dairy product.

Scoop the batter into the prepared pan and smooth the top. Lay a sheet of tinfoil loosely over the top and bake for 50 minutes. Remove the foil and bake for an additional 10–15 minutes. Allow to cool before serving.

Mandy's Savoury Cheese & Herb Bread

This recipe produces a delicious savoury quick bread! Loaded with eggs and cheese, it is both satisfying and satiating. Perfect for breakfast, added to lunchboxes, or paired with a glass of wine—the possibilities are endless! Halloumi and mint are classic Cypriot flavours, though you can use any combination of grated hard cheeses (cheddar, Gouda, Emmental) and herbs (spring onions, parsley, basil). This versatile loaf allows you to play with different flavour combinations—think olives, jalapenos, or spicy European chorizo! A big thank you to my friend Mandy Caldis, who introduced me to this bread!

FLAVOUR NOTE: You can be creative with your additions, creating a variety of breads featuring delicious combinations. But do take care not to overcrowd the flavours.

MAKES 2 SMALL LOAVES OR 1 VERY LARGE LOAF

500 g / 4 cups all-purpose or bread flour
15 g / 3 tsp baking powder
7 g / 1 tsp salt
250 g / 1 cup buttermilk or Greek yogurt
6 eggs (beaten)
220 g / 1 cup butter (melted) or mild olive oil
250 g / 3 cups grated halloumi (or cheese of your choice)
12 g / ½ cup fresh mint (finely chopped) or 8 g / ¼ cup dried mint (pulverized)

Alternative additions

90–100 g / ½ cup olives (pitted and chopped)
80 g / ½ cup raisins (soaked and drained)
52 g / ½ cup spring onions (chopped)
10 g / ½ cup basil leaves (chopped)
30 g / ½ cup sun-dried tomatoes (chopped)
45 g / ½ cup jalapeños (sliced)
100 g / ½ cup cooked bacon, chorizo, or pepperoni (sliced)
1 g / 1½ tsp garlic or onion powder

Preheat the oven to 350°F. Grease a large Pullman pan, standard Bundt pan, or 2 8 ½-inch loaf pans with butter. (Two disposable 900 g / 2 pound loaf pans will work well too!)

Combine the dry ingredients in a large bowl and mix briefly.

In a medium bowl, whisk together the buttermilk, eggs, and butter (or oil). Add the liquid ingredients, cheese, and herbs to the dry ingredients and gently fold together until no dry flour is visible. Transfer the batter to the prepared pan(s).

Bake in the preheated oven for 55–60 minutes, or until a toothpick stuck into the centre comes out clean. Let the savoury loaf rest for 15–20 minutes, then gently turn it out of the pan and onto a cooling rack.

Vegan Banana Bread

This loaf regularly featured at my full-day bread workshops at my bakery in South Africa. When you are catering for large groups, it is always a good idea to have a vegan option or two up your sleeve. This banana bread is simple and delicious. I doubt you will even miss the dairy or eggs!

NOTE: If you want to make a small banana loaf, be sure to halve the recipe!

MAKES 1 EXTRA-LARGE OR 2 SMALL LOAVES

300 g / 2 ¼ cups all-purpose or bread flour
75 g / ½ cup spelt flour
5 g / tsp baking soda
13 g / 2 ¾ tsp baking powder
1 g / ¼ tsp salt (good pinch)
2 g / ¾ tsp cinnamon
185 g / 1 cup brown sugar
200 g / 1 cup liquid coconut or sunflower (or other mild) oil
600 g / 2 cups bananas (mashed)
120 g / ¾ cup nuts or dates (chopped, optional)

Preheat the oven to 350°F. Grease a large loaf pan (a large Pullman works well) or 2 medium loaf pans.

Combine the flours, baking soda, baking powder, salt, and cinnamon in a medium bowl and mix together briefly. In another medium bowl, combine the sugar and oil and mix well. Add the mashed bananas to the oil and sugar and fold in. Slowly add the flour mixture to the wet ingredients and stir well. Fold in the nuts or dates (if using).

Spoon the batter into the prepared pan(s), and bake in the preheated oven for 60–70 minutes, or until a toothpick comes out clean.

Oumie's Buttermilk Rusks (Karringmelk Beskuit) 233
Bread Rusks 235
Grissini 237
Guilty Conscience Crackers 239
Bruna's Egg Pasta 241

Breads for the Pantry

There is something very reassuring about a well-stocked pantry or larder. An unspoken promise of sustenance, nourishment, and survival. And when it comes to pantry staples you are not limited to rice, legumes, grains, and cereals. Dehydrated foods such as rusks, grissini, crackers, and pasta make an excellent addition to your list of homemade shelf-stable groceries.

The practice of food preservation is multifaceted. Some foods are salted and cured, while others are fermented, frozen, or dried. Dehydration protects foods from contamination and spoilage caused by harmful bacteria. For early seafarers and voyagers, dry, hard biscuits were common fare. Twice-baked or dehydrated on low heat for an extended period of time, these foods could be stored for months or even years.

It is no surprise, then, that rusks, or sailors' hardtack, remained in use long after the first European settlers arrived in the Cape. Later, throughout the Great Trek of the Voortrekkers—the Boer (farmer) communities of Dutch, German, and French descent, who migrated away from the Cape Colony deeper into the South African interior—they were still an essential food. Rusks have undoubtedly become a South African staple and are deeply ingrained within the country's food heritage and psyche. Today they are enjoyed with tea or coffee (especially for breakfast) or as an anytime snack throughout the day.

Traditional, naturally leavened bread rusks were made with buttermilk and spiced with aniseed. These rusks are less sweet than the more modern cake rusks, which are chemically leavened. Despite the increase in popularity of sweet rusks, the old-fashioned yeast-leavened rusks have a longer shelf life than their contemporary cousins. They are similar to the Dutch beschuit and Greek paximadia.

Most breads and plain cakes can be turned into rusks. Simply allow them to cool completely before cutting (or breaking) them into smaller portions. Transfer the pieces to a large baking sheet lined with parchment paper and bake on low heat until dry. Allow to cool completely before transferring to an airtight container.

Oumie's Buttermilk Rusks (Karringmelk Beskuit)

Whenever we visited my oumie's (grandmother's) house as children, we would rush to open the large yellow cake tin she always kept well stocked with freshly baked treats. Sometimes we would find a large date and coffee cake or a mountain of jam tertjies (tarts), though few things would get us quite as excited as the discovery of a full tin of Oumie's buttermilk rusks!

MAKES 1 VERY LARGE TIN OF RUSKS

1 kg / 8 cups cake or all-purpose flour
280–300 g / 1 ½ cups sugar
7 g / 1 tsp fine sea salt
30–35 g / 7 tsp baking powder
180 g / 2 cups desiccated coconut (optional)
120 g / 1 cup wheat bran (optional)
500 mL / 2 cups buttermilk (room temperature)
3 eggs (beaten)
500 g / 2 ¼ cups butter (melted)

Preheat the oven to 355°F. Line a ¾ sheet pan (or 2 half-sheet pans) with parchment paper.

Combine all the dry ingredients in a large bowl. Add buttermilk and eggs, and gently fold into the flour mixture. Add the melted butter and work into a soft dough. To do this, you will gently knead or massage the dough by hand. Be careful not to overwork the dough, as the resulting rusks will be dense instead of light and crumbly.

Transfer the dough to the prepared baking sheet(s) making sure to spread it evenly over the whole sheet—your trusty dough scraper (page 13) will come in handy here!

Bake in the preheated oven for 30–35 minutes, until golden. Allow to cool completely before slicing into desired rusk sizes.

Preheat the oven to 210°F.

Gently arrange the rusks on 2 or more baking sheets and bake until completely dry.

Now based in Canada, I restock that very same age-worn tin (pictured here) with freshly baked rusks on a monthly basis. A treasured family tradition that connects me to my grandmother and to South Africa. To where I come from and to those who came before.

Bread Rusks

The concept of dehydrating or toasting bread (whether for long preservation or shortly before serving) is found within many culinary traditions around the world. Scandinavian crispbread, Greek paximadia, Italian biscotti, and Dutch beschuit are only a few examples of breads that are intentionally dried to produce rusks or crackers. They can be eaten dry, topped with delicious toppings, or rehydrated by soaking in tea, coffee, wine, water, or olive oil. These breads are also well suited to being served with a hearty soup or stew, and will soak up the delicious gravy or sauce like a sponge.

These rusks are easy to make and are very versatile. You can even use store-bought bread to make them! Bread rolls and buns should be sliced open and the halves (or thirds) placed on a baking sheet lined with parchment paper. Slices of sandwich bread or French loaves can be arranged in the same way. Bagels, koulouria, and quick breads such as the Wholemeal Soda Bread (page 223) can be cut into thin slices and dehydrated on low heat.

Bake at 210°F until dry, approximately 3–5 hours (depending on the type of bread and thickness of the slices). Once dry, allow the rusks to cool completely and then transfer to an airtight container or glass jar, where they can be stored for 2–3 months.

You can enjoy your homemade bread rusks for breakfast, topped with butter and hagelslag (Dutch chocolate sprinkles) or cheese and jam. Alternatively, you can turn them into Italian panzanella salad, French tartines, or Greek dakos. These crunchy treats can also be served with a variety of dips or delicious pâtés. For more ideas on what to do with old dry bread and rusks, have a look at the recipes in the next chapter.

Grissini

Like rusks, grissini (or breadsticks) can be made from most any bread dough, though firm (low-hydration) doughs are easiest to work with. Sesame grissini are my all-time favourite—the perfect snack with coffee and a great utensil to scoop up flavourful dips and spreads. Hugely popular in Italy and Greece, these crunchy treats are guaranteed to win you over!

MAKES 25–30 BREADSTICKS

1 batch Government Loaf dough (page 67)
Sesame seeds, for topping (optional)

Prepare the dough as per the recipe instructions. When the dough has bulk fermented for a minimum of 2 hours, it is ready to be shaped into breadsticks.

Line a baking sheet with parchment paper.

Divide the dough into 25–30 equal pieces (approximately 30 g / 1 oz) each. Use approximately 1 teaspoon of sesame seeds per piece of dough and roll them into 12–16-inch sticks. To do this, start rolling the dough with one hand. Do not flour the countertop, as this will cause the dough to slip and slide instead of rolling and stretching. Once the piece of dough starts to lengthen, add the teaspoon of sesame seeds to the countertop and continue rolling and stretching the dough, pressing and coaxing the seeds to stick to the surface of the breadstick. Some of the seeds may disappear into the dough instead of remaining on the outside, which only adds to the overall sesame flavour!

Transfer the breadsticks to the prepared baking sheet(s), leaving about ½ inch between each piece. Loosely cover with cling film (to prevent them from drying out). Allow the grissini to rise for 40–60 minutes, until doubled in size.

Preheat the oven to 390°F.

Bake the grissini for 15–20 minutes, or until golden brown. Allow the breadsticks to cool.

For crunchy breadsticks, preheat the oven to low heat (210°F) and return the cooled grissini to the oven and dehydrate (bake) until completely dry.

Allow the dry grissini to cool before transferring them to an airtight container.

Guilty Conscience Crackers

Love them or hate them, sourdough discard recipes are here to stay. The internet is inundated with creative ideas on how to use up excess starter—some better than others! Let's face it, sometimes life takes an unexpected turn and you end up with more sourdough starter than you need. Enter discard crackers, a delicious and practical alternative to washing your precious starter down the drain. If you don't have a sourdough starter but still want to give these crackers a go, you can use a poolish pre-ferment (page 91) instead.

TIPS: If you are using a poolish pre-ferment, be sure to start it the day before you want to make the crackers. You can also allow the cracker dough to rest in the fridge for 2–3 days before rolling out and baking your crackers. This will result in extra flavourful (slightly tangy) crackers.

This recipe produces a large batch of crackers, and for good reason. You can, of course, halve the recipe, but if you are going to the trouble of making crackers, you might as well make enough. These store well, but they are decidedly moreish and will disappear before you know it!

MAKES 1 LARGE BATCH OF CRACKERS

130 g water (or a little more for dry dough)
250 g / 1 cup sourdough discard or poolish pre-ferment
95 g / ½ cup olive oil or butter (melted)
2.4 g / 2 tsp dried rosemary (optional)
11 g / 1 ¾ tsp salt
250 g / 2 cups white bread or all-purpose flour
250 g / 2 cups whole-wheat or spelt flour
Black and white sesame seeds, poppy seeds, coarse sea salt, or everything bagel seasoning (optional topping)

In a large bowl, combine the water, starter (sourdough discard or pre-ferment), oil or butter, herbs, and salt and whisk together. Gradually add the flour and work into a dough. It will be quite firm and sticky (not overly wet). Knead briefly, until all the ingredients are well incorporated and the dough consistency is somewhat homogenous. (Only add flour to the counter if the dough is still sticky after 5–10 minutes of kneading.) Shape the dough into a ball, cover, and allow to rest at room temperature for 3–4 hours, or in the fridge overnight.

Preheat the oven to 350°F. Line a baking sheet with parchment paper.

Divide the dough into 4 pieces. Return 3 of the 4 pieces to the bowl and cover them so they do not dry out. Scatter the seeds (if using) over the surface of the dough and press them in slightly. Use a rolling pin or pasta machine to roll the dough out as thinly as possible (approximately 1–2 mm thick).

Cut the dough into shapes of your choice using a knife, bench scraper, cookie cutter, or the rim of a glass. (Round crackers will take significantly longer to make than square crackers, as they have to be cut out one by one.)

Gently transfer the cut pieces to the prepared baking sheet. Pierce (dock) the cracker dough all over with a fork to prevent the crackers from puffing up while baking.

For a rustic, hassle-free cracker alternative, you can roll out the dough in the same way and place the whole piece on the prepared baking sheet and pierce with a fork. You will break it into pieces once it is baked and cooled.

Bake in the preheated oven for 20–25 minutes, until the edges just start to turn golden. Be careful not to overbake these, they burn quickly! Once the first batch of crackers are baked, transfer them to a cooling rack and continue baking the rest of the crackers in batches until all the dough is used up. This may take some time. If necessary, you can split the baking process over 2 days.

Cool and store in an airtight container.

POOLISH PRE-FERMENT

125 g flour
125 g water
Pinch of instant yeast

Combine all ingredients together, cover, and allow to sit overnight.

Bruna's Egg Pasta

This beautifully simple Italian staple food is produced from unleavened dough with eggs and cooked by boiling or baking (such as in lasagna). Fellow South African foodie and pasta-making expert, Bruna Green (née Perotti), very generously shared her family's egg pasta recipe with me. Bruna and her mother, Clara, were born in Ripatransone, a tiny village on the top of a hill in the Marche region of Central Italy—a village with eight churches, where in Bruna's words, "the bells told the time and the stories of daily living."

TIPS: The quantity of flour is just a guideline, depending on the size of the eggs, the humidity in the air, and how much egg the flour absorbs.

Doppio zero flour (also known as 00 flour) is a finely ground high protein Italian flour and is commonly used to make pizza and pasta dough.

VARIATIONS: This pasta dough can be used to make lasagna sheets, tagliatelle, or filled pastas such as ravioli.

SERVES 4

400 g / 3 ¼ cups doppio zero flour or high-protein bread flour (plus more for dusting)
4 eggs
Semolina flour or additional doppio zero flour (for dusting)

Place a mound of flour on a large wooden board or kitchen counter and make a well in the centre. Break the eggs into the well. Using a fork, beat the eggs and, little by little, start incorporating the flour into the egg mixture. When the ingredients start to come together, set the fork aside and get ready to use your hands (or a spatula).

Push some of the flour to one side—it is quite possible you will not use it all. Keep adding small quantities of flour to the egg mixture. Continue mixing (with your hands or the spatula), folding, and adding flour until the dough is no longer sticky. Once most of the flour has been absorbed into a shaggy dough, it is time to knead.

Use the palms of your hands to knead the dough. Keep kneading for 10–15 minutes, adding flour as necessary and until the dough is smooth and elastic. If the dough springs back when prodded, the consistency is correct. Wrap the dough in cling film and leave it to rest for 20–30 minutes. You can also place the dough in the fridge overnight (but no longer than 24 hours). Allow it to come to room temperature the next day, before rolling it out.

Before you roll out the dough, make sure to read the instructions that came with your pasta machine.

You are ready to roll!

Divide your pasta dough in half. Wrap one piece in clingfilm and set aside until needed. Stretch the piece of dough into a slight oval (using your hands or a rolling pin) and lightly dust with flour. Set your pasta machine to the widest setting (usually No. 1) and carefully start feeding the dough through the machine. Once the entire piece of dough has gone through the machine, reduce the width by a setting. Feed the sheet of dough through the machine again then reduce the width by an additional setting. Once the dough has gone through the machine on the third setting, fold the sheet over itself 3–4 times (equal pieces). Roll the layers together gently using a rolling pin, then return to your pasta machine. Again set the pasta machine to the widest setting (No. 1) and feed the layered pasta dough through the machine. Once it is through, set the machine to the second setting and continue feeding the dough through the machine on the different settings until the desired thickness is reached. Cut into sheets of 10–12 inches, dust with 00 or semolina flour and allow to dry for 30 minutes (until slightly leathery) before cutting into linguine, pappardelle, or fettuccine. Repeat with the remaining piece of dough.

The fresh pasta can be dried on a pasta drying rack and stored in a brown paper bag or wrapped in a kitchen towel. Alternatively, toss it in a bit of semolina flour and place it in freezer bags and freeze (use within 2–3 months).

Fresh homemade pasta cooks in 3–4 minutes. Dried homemade pasta needs 1–2 minutes longer.

Serve hot with a simple sauce or a generous drizzle of olive oil, shavings of parmesan, and freshly ground salt and black pepper—and perhaps some chili flakes.

> **"A plate of homemade pasta, a glass of wine, some gentle Italian music, a little grappa with your espresso, time with special people, make life beautiful . . . Si, la vita e bella."—Bruna**

Ioannis Kourelos's Skordalia (Greek Garlic & Bread Dip) 247

Mama Mou's Garlic Bread 249

Gérard's French Toast (Pain Perdu) 250

BBQ Toasted Sandwiches (Braaibroodjies) 251

Gogo's Turkey Stuffing 252

Breadcrumbs 255

Old Bread

At the time of writing an estimated 1.3 billion tonnes of food is wasted globally each year. Nine hundred thousand tonnes of this is bread. These are large-scale problems to which I do not have the answers. On a small scale, however, in the domestic realm, I have a few ideas about how to curb your bread wastage by creatively repurposing old bread in simple and decidedly delicious ways. And you are not limited to croutons, breadcrumbs, and bread pudding, though those are great too!

In this chapter, I offer some of my favourite recipes for using up old, dry, or staling bread. Loaves that have lost their softness and moisture (but have not gone mouldy) can be useful and nifty ingredients in the kitchen! And with only a little planning and foresight, you will never have to discard a single piece of bread again. Read on to find a selection of clever, thrifty, and frugal ways to prevent bread wastage in your kitchen.

Ioannis Kourelos's Skordalia (Greek Garlic & Bread Dip)

The Greeks are known for their delicious and diverse meze—small plates of savoury snacks and dips. But where much of the world is familiar with hummus, tzatziki, and tahini, skordalia is the lesser known relative. This delicious dip is made with plenty of garlic (skordo / σκόρδο) and thickened with either bread, potato, or nuts. In Greece it is customary to serve this garlicky dish with fish or vegetables. Alternatively, skordalia can be enjoyed with other meze. Here follows my late father-in-law Ioannis Kourelos's skordalia recipe.

TIP: It is best to avoid using a strong olive oil in this recipe, as it will dominate and upset the balance of flavours.

3 slices day-old white bread
2–3 cloves garlic (or more to taste)
1 small potato (peeled and boiled)
53 g / 4 Tbsp mild olive oil or vegetable oil* (to bind)
Salt, pepper, and lemon juice, to taste

**You may need a little more oil, depending on how thirsty the mixture is (thickness of bread and size of potato).*

Remove the crusts from the bread and place the slices in a small bowl. Pour a little water over the bread—just enough to cover—and set aside to soak for 5 minutes.

Finely grate or crush the garlic.

Squeeze the water from the bread and place it in a food processor along with the boiled potato and the garlic. Add a good glug of oil and slowly process until the ingredients are well combined. Steadily add more oil and continue to blend until the mixture is smooth and has a light, creamy appearance (but not runny). Season with salt and pepper, add a generous squeeze of lemon juice, and mix well. Taste and add more salt, pepper, or lemon juice, if necessary.

Serve this garlicky masterpiece as part of your next grazing board or harvest table.

Mama Mou's Garlic Bread

It goes without saying that homemade garlic bread is far superior to the store-bought variety. But if you didn't bake the bread yourself, at least prepare your own garlic butter!

In our family, a single loaf of garlic bread never seems to cut it. Luckily, my mother's recipe (μαμά μου = my mother) produces enough garlic butter for two large French loaves/baguettes—and perhaps a tad extra! By all means double or triple this recipe to your heart's content. It's an excellent way to repurpose stale French loaves! Serve warm as a side to braaied (grilled) meat and salad or a beautiful bowl of tomato soup.

NOTE: This bread can also be baked on the BBQ.

- 2 Baguettes with Poolish (page 91) or store-bought French loaves
- 300 g / 1 ¼ cups + 2 Tbsp salted butter (softened)
- 4–5 cloves garlic (finely chopped)
- 2–3 Tbsp fresh parsley (finely chopped)
- Salt and black pepper (freshly ground), to taste

Preheat the oven to 355°F.

Slice the baguette into generous ½-inch slices—but make sure not to sever the pieces completely.

Combine the remaining ingredients in a small bowl and mix well.

Spread a generous amount of the garlic butter between the slices. Any excess can be spread over the top of the loaf or used to add flavour to sauces or stews.

Wrap the bread in tinfoil and bake in the preheated oven for 15–20 minutes. Allow to cool for 5 minutes before unwrapping. Enjoy!

Gérard's French Toast (Pain Perdu)

Gérard's neighbours would regularly pass by the bakery just as the baker was pulling his signature loaves out of the sturdy masonry oven. Large jars of thick, creamy yogurt or bunches of fresh asparagus would often be exchanged for a hefty bâtard. And whenever there was a delivery of farm eggs, Gérard would make pain perdu—lost bread. Truth be told, I never much cared for French toast, but Gérard's version was an easy sell. Thick slices of day-old sourdough soaked in cream, dusted with maple sugar, and fried in butter. What's not to like?

SERVES 4

- 3–4 eggs
- 6–8 slices of day-old sourdough bread
- 250 mL / 9 oz cream
- 100 g / ½ cup maple sugar or light brown sugar
- Butter for frying

In a small, low-rimmed bowl, beat the eggs and set aside.

Briefly soak the bread in the cream, turning the slices over so both sides soak up a good amount of cream (but be careful not to let the bread become too soggy).

Put a pan on to heat and add enough butter to properly coat the base of the pan.

Working quickly, transfer the cream-soaked slices to the bowl of beaten eggs (again turning the slices over).

One by one, coat each slice in maple sugar (a flat plate or low-rimmed bowl will work well here).

Fry in the hot butter until cooked through and beautifully caramelized on both sides.

Enjoy with berries, sour cream, and a generous drizzle of maple syrup.

BBQ Toasted Sandwiches (Braaibroodjies)

Braaibroodjies are essentially toasted sandwiches that are grilled over a fire. The fillings vary, from cheese, onion, and tomato, to sweet chili sauce, cold meats, mustard, mayonnaise, and sun-dried tomatoes. For added moisture and flavour, make sure to butter the bread on both sides before assembling the sandwiches. Although adding cheese to braaibroodjies is quite common, this was not the norm in our household, and at the risk of being somewhat controversial, I must admit that I prefer the cheeseless version. But whatever fillings you decide on, do not skimp on the butter!

TIP: These are closed sandwiches so plan for a minimum of 2 slices per person, plus a few extras for good measure!

Slices of 2–3-day-old bread
Salted butter (softened)
Tomatoes (thinly sliced)
Onion (thinly sliced into rings)
Salt and pepper

Butter the slices of bread on both sides (yes, it is allowed). Set aside half the slices—these will be used to close the sandwiches once you have added the fillings.

Place 2–3 slices of tomato on each slice of bread, followed by a few slices of the thinly sliced onion. Season with salt and pepper and close with another buttered slice.

Continue making the sandwiches and stack them on a breadboard or plate, ready to be presented to the person manning the fire.

Preheat the grill (or allow the fire to die down) to medium-low heat.

Place the sandwiches in a foldable gridiron (grill basket) and grill, turning often to ensure even grilling. The braaibroodjies are ready when they are beautifully golden and boast a couple of grill lines. Serve as a side to grilled meat, salad and vegetables, or your usual BBQ menu.

Gogo's Turkey Stuffing

My step-grandmother, Sheelagh Roome (née Coalter), was raised in the KwaZulu-Natal Midlands in South Africa. Born to English and Irish parents but growing up in the heart of Zululand, she learned to speak Zulu before she could speak English, and today insists on being called Gogo instead of Granny. Gogo's stuffing recipe is wonderfully versatile. It can be cooked in separate loaf pans or inside the turkey where it can absorb the beautiful juices and flavours of the roasting meat. And the secret to a superb stuffing? Stale bread, top-quality bangers (pork sausages), and plenty of fresh herbs!

TIP: Stuffing baked inside a whole turkey will remain moist, but stuffing baked in a loaf pan can become a little dry. To avoid this, add a little olive oil, liquid chicken stock, or a beaten egg to keep it moist.

SERVES 8–10 AS A SIDE DISH

- 30 g / 2 ⅛ Tbsp butter
- 2 onions (finely chopped)
- 1 celery stalk (chopped)
- 800 g–1 kg / 1.7–2.2 lb pork sausages (skins removed)
- Breadcrumbs (page 255) from 4–5 slices stale bread
- 1–2 g / 1 Tbsp fresh sage (chopped)
- 1 g / ½ Tbsp fresh thyme (chopped)
- Salt and pepper, to taste
- 1 egg, olive oil, or liquid chicken stock (optional)

In a pan, use the butter to sauté the onions and celery briefly and remove from the heat.

Crumble the pork sausages into a large bowl. Add the breadcrumbs, fresh herbs, onions, and celery. Season with a little salt and pepper and mix well.

If you are baking the stuffing in a separate pan, you can mix in an egg or a little olive oil or chicken stock (broth) to keep it moist before transferring it to a greased pan.

Stuffing baked inside a turkey will have the same cooking time as the turkey. Stuffing baked in a loaf pan should be covered with tinfoil and placed in the oven during the last 40–45 minutes of the turkey's cooking time.

Serve the stuffing as a side to your Christmas or Thanksgiving meal.

Babette's bread
RASURKULTUR

Breadcrumbs

If you are looking for additional inspiration, consider turning your old bread into breadcrumbs and use them to make savoury baked vegetable crumbles or crumbed chicken, fish fingers, or croquettes. Homemade breadcrumbs can also be used as part of the filling for sausage rolls, meatballs, and burger patties. Or perhaps you would enjoy a Spanish gazpacho or Greek melitzanosalata (eggplant dip). The possibilities are endless!

Stale bread, bread rusks, or crackers (or briefly toast a few pieces of bread in a toaster or oven)

If using a cheese grater, carefully grate the pieces of dry bread until you have the desired amount of breadcrumbs.

If using a blender, break the bread into smaller chunks before blending. Pulse until the desired texture is reached (coarse or fine).

Store your homemade breadcrumbs in an airtight container for 2–3 weeks or freeze them in a Ziploc bag for up to 3 months.

NOTE: You can flavour your breadcrumbs with grated parmesan, herbs, spices, or everything bagel seasoning, though any oils or fats (eg. olive oil or parmesan) will shorten the shelf life of your breadcrumbs.

Follow the Breadcrumbs

Bread baking, like any craft, requires patience, practice, and skill. It is normal to feel a little lost and uncertain when starting out on your bread-baking journey. Everything will feel foreign, odd, and a little uncomfortable, but it will get easier. For this reason, I have laid a trail of breadcrumbs in the form of useful tips, tricks, and ideas to help you find your way.

In this chapter, you will find a list of additions and inclusions (and suggestions for when to add them to your dough) as well as ideas on how best to store your bread.

You will also find a section on common bread-baking problems (and their solutions) and a few notes about fitting bread-baking into your schedule. These are guidelines, not hard and fast rules. I encourage you to adapt them to suit your unique baking circumstances and needs.

With enough practice, you will soon find your own way.

Additions & inclusions

Adding seeds, nuts, fruits, herbs, cheeses, and so on to your bread is a wonderful way to enhance its flavour and overall texture, making it even more special. Adding whole grains and seeds also ups the fibre content and nutritional value of the bread. As you will have gathered from the diverse selection of recipes in this book, not all additions are treated the same way. Some ingredients need to be soaked prior to being added to the dough, while others are added only during the final shaping stage.

Below you will find a list of wonderful bread additions, as well as suggestions on how to treat them and when to add them.

- SEEDS: Soak in water overnight, then add them to the dough after the first hour of bulk fermentation. Drain the seeds prior to mixing the dough and use any excess soaking water as part of the overall hydration required by the recipe.
- WHOLE AND CRUSHED GRAINS: Same process as the seeds (see above).
- NUTS: No soaking required, simply add to the dough after the first hour of bulk fermentation.
- RAISINS, CURRANTS, SULTANAS, CANDIED CITRUS PEEL: Soak in water, mild tea (like rooibos), orange juice, rum, or brandy (excess soaking liquid can be discarded or used as part of the overall hydration in the recipe). Add after the first hour of bulk fermentation or during final shaping.
- OLIVES: Make sure to remove the pits. No soaking required. Add after the first hour of bulk fermentation.
- ROASTED GARLIC: Add during final shaping.
- HARD CHEESE: Add chunky squares after the first hour of bulk fermentation or during final shaping.
- SOFT CHEESE: Add during final shaping.
- CHOCOLATE CHIPS: Add during final shaping.
- JALAPEÑOS/CHILIES: Add during final shaping.
- SUN-DRIED TOMATOES: Add after the first hour of bulk fermentation or during final shaping.
- SPICES: Add when mixing dry ingredients together.
- DRIED HERBS: Add when mixing dry ingredients together or during final shaping.
- FRESH HERBS: Add during initial mixing phase or sprinkle on top of the bread (eg. Focaccia) in the last five minutes of baking.

Storing, freezing & defrosting bread

Fresh bread can be kept on a breadboard on your kitchen counter for one to two days. Once sliced, place the bread slice-side down onto the breadboard.

Bread that is a few days old should be kept in a linen or paper bread bag or a bread tin.

Avoid storing your bread in the fridge, as this will cause the starches in the bread to recrystallize, causing the bread to go stale faster.

Avoid storing your bread in plastic, especially during hot and humid months. The plastic will cause the bread to sweat, which in turn will cause the bread to go mouldy.

Any excess bread should be frozen on the day of baking (once cooled). When freezing bread, wrap the loaves tightly in cling film to prevent freezer burn and use within two to three weeks. (Consider slicing the loaf prior to wrapping in plastic. Frozen slices can be popped in the toaster for easy defrosting.) Defrost whole loaves at room temperature overnight for use the next day. To refresh the crust, heat the loaf at 350°F for five to ten minutes.

Excess bread may also be turned into bread rusks (page 235).

Troubleshooting

You tried your best to keep the dough happy, but something went wrong. Below you will find a list of common bread-baking issues, along with ideas on how to prevent future mishaps.

- **FORGOT TO ADD THE SALT?**

  If you have not baked the bread yet, sprinkle some of the salt over the surface of the dough and gently massage it in. Repeat until all the salt has been added and equally distributed.

  If the bread was baked without salt, turn the loaf into garlic bread or garlic croutons—the strong flavours will mask the lack of salt.

- **GOOD SHAPE BUT DENSE INSIDE**

  The dough was under-proofed or too little water was used to mix it. Allow for a slightly longer final rise next time round (don't rush the dough!) and perhaps try increasing the hydration slightly.

- **FLAT AND DENSE BREAD**

  The dough over-proofed prior to baking. Reshape over-proofed dough prior to baking and allow for a slightly shorter final rise. (NOTE: Sourdough cannot be reshaped.)

- **THE LOAF PANCAKED AND FLATTENED OUTWARDS**

  Insufficient gluten strength. Either the flour was too weak, the dough was not worked enough (not enough stretches and folds), or too much water (hydration) was added.

- **BREAD COLLAPSED**

  The dough over-proofed during the final rise or the oven temperature was too low.

- **OVERLY STICKY DOUGH THAT CAN'T BE SHAPED**

  The dough over-fermented. The gluten structure has completely broken down and become weak to the point where it cannot hold its shape. The dough may be baked in a loaf pan but will yield a dense and rather heavy loaf.

- **BREAD DIDN'T RISE**

  The yeast expired or the immediate environment (room) was too cold. It is also possible that the salt and yeast came into direct contact and that the yeast was weakened (burned) by the salt.

- **OVERLY PALE BREAD**

  The dough was over-kneaded (overmixed) or over-fermented (depleted sugars) and unable to caramelize properly.

- **OVERLY FIRM/HARD DOUGH THAT CAN'T BE SHAPED**

  The dough was overmixed. This is unlikely to happen when mixing and folding by hand *but* very common when mixing in a stand mixer. Use the slowest setting and do not rush the dough.

- **TRIANGULAR (PYRAMID-SHAPED) BREAD**

  The dough was under-fermented and the yeast was not yet properly active. Try allowing the dough more time next time round.

- **WET AND SLOPPY DOUGH WITH TOO MUCH ADDED WATER**

  Bake the dough in a greased loaf pan. The sides of the pan will provide support to the weak dough and allow it to rise. Alternatively, transfer the dough to a baking sheet and bake as a flatbread.

- **LARGE HOLES AND TUNNELS THROUGHOUT THE LOAF**

  Poor shaping technique or inconsistent heat and steam while baking.

- **FLYING CRUST THAT CAME AWAY FROM THE REST OF THE BREAD LEAVING A GAPING HOLE**

  Poor shaping technique or the dough over-fermented. Be more careful when shaping and try shortening the final rising time.

- **GUMMY ON THE BOTTOM**

  Insufficient heat (oven too cool) or the dough over-proofed prior to baking.

- **BURST, LOPSIDED, EXPLODED, UNEVEN BREAD**

  Poor shaping, shallow scoring, under-proofed dough, or inadequate steam while baking.

- **UNSIGHTLY LINES AND LAYERS OF FLOUR INSIDE THE LOAF**

  Too much flour was used and folded into the dough while shaping. Gently brush excess flour from the dough when shaping your loaves.

- **CUTS (SCORING) IN THE DOUGH DID NOT OPEN UP PROPERLY**

  Firm doughs can be scored more deeply. Weaker, softer, wetter doughs should receive shallow cuts. Adequate steam should also be applied during the first fifteen to twenty minutes of baking.

- **DENSE CRUMB WITH THE OCCASIONAL LARGE BUBBLE/GAPING HOLE**

  Underproofed dough. Try extending the bulk fermentation time until the dough is light, puffy, and a little jiggly before moving on to shaping. Alternatively, allow for an extended final fermentation once shaped.

Fitting bread baking into your schedule

Baking bread is fun and incredibly rewarding, but it does involve a bit of planning. When you don't have much time but still want to bake or you have run out of bread and need to put something on the table in a hurry, opt for a simple straight dough bread (page 61) or a quick bread (page 219).

On weekends, or when you happen to have a little more time on your hands, start expanding your baking repertoire and try your hand at some of the more time-consuming (but definitely worthwhile) recipes in this book.

Don't over-complicate things by skipping over the instructions. Be sure to read the entire recipe before you start mixing your dough and make sure you have enough hours left in the day to finish baking your loaves, so you don't end up baking in the middle of the night! If you are going to make time to bake, take a few extra minutes to understand what the recipe entails and properly plan your bake (or choose a different recipe).

The best way to plan your bake is to decide when you want the bread to be ready and to check how long (give or take) the specific bread will take to make. Then work backwards to determine when you should start making your dough. Some bread doughs can be placed in the fridge after the first hour of bulk fermentation and used the following day. (Remember to let the dough come to room temperature before shaping.) Other doughs will require several hours at room temperature before being shaped.

Choose a recipe and make it a few times, tweaking and perfecting as you learn. And once you have baked a couple of loaves and started to get a feel for the process, try making a double batch—one loaf for the kitchen counter and one for the freezer. (You'll thank yourself later!)

Final Thoughts & Recommendations

Start with the basics. Once you are comfortable with the ins and outs of a simple sandwich loaf or basic country loaf, the rest of the recipes in the book will be easy to master. Remember that the recipe is intended to guide but should not always be followed to a T. Pay special attention to the following things and adjust as necessary:

- WATER: The amount of water will need to be adjusted according to the type of flour you are using (absorbency and protein) and the level of moisture and humidity in the air (for example, rainy day).

  The water temperature will also need to be adjusted according to the season (is it winter or summer?) or the ambient temperature in your kitchen.

- OVEN/BAKING TEMP: No oven is the same. Drawing from your own experience with the behaviour of your oven, you may need to increase or decrease the temperature accordingly.
- BAKING TIME: As a general rule, smaller loaves (rolls) and long, thin breads (like baguettes) will require less baking time. Large, heavy, and whole-grain loaves are best baked a little longer. When in doubt, allow 5–10 minutes extra baking time. (If the loaf is darkening too much, lay a sheet of foil loosely over the top.) The baking time will also depend on what colour and texture of the crust you desire.
- FERMENTATION TIME: Fermentation time will change with the weather and the seasons as well as the temperature of your kitchen. Warmer temperatures will accelerate and shorten the fermentation time. Conversely, cooler temperatures will slow down the yeast and result in longer fermentation times.

Snippets from the bakery in Maboneng.

Acknowledgements

This book truly is the achievement of an international team of creative professionals. A big thank you to Emily Lycopolus for your generous advice and pivotal introductions. To Taryn Boyd, for seeing potential in my book proposal. To Tori Elliott, my publisher, for taking over the reins and for pushing me out of my comfort zone. To my editors Kate Kennedy, Marial Shea, and Senica Maltese, for whittling this book into shape. To Danielle Acken for your creative input and gorgeous photography. To Aurelia Louvet for your irresistible food styling. To Karené Wedekind, for your kindness and stunning photography. To Annalize Nel, for your warmth and beautiful images. To Alon Skuy for your wonderful photography. To River Makings, for your artistic eye and magnificent photography. To Sarah de Roche for your friendship and handsome photography. To Willemijn Schellekens, for your creative vision and for breathing fresh air into the Babette's Bread logo and corporate identity. To Jazmin Welch for your innovative and attractive designs. A huge thank you to you all!

Saying that one is going to write a book and actually writing a book are two very different things. I take my hat off to every published author out there. Completing a manuscript is no mean feat and gives even a law degree a run for its money!

I have always wanted to write but seem to have gone about it in a somewhat roundabout way. Then again, to write, one needs something to write about, a valuable notion my stepfather, Kevin, shared with me many years before I attended university. Engaging stories and interesting content cannot be pulled from thin air. Good stories come from facing life head on, from doing, feeling, questioning, and experiencing. From travelling to other countries, being exposed to foreign cultures, and learning new skills (and languages)! These are the things that add colour to our lives and make for stories (and recipes) that are worth sharing.

I am incredibly grateful to my parents for providing my sisters and me with a worldly upbringing. For encouraging us to read widely, to pursue our interests, to learn to play musical instruments, and to get a degree (even if we don't practise what we studied). A special thank you goes out to my mother, Theodora, for always being with me even when we are far apart, for knowing when I need a little extra push, and for allowing me to pursue a career in baking. To my stepfather, Kevin, for suggesting I bake something other than cakes and cookies, and for helping me set up that first home bakery and designing the original Babette's Bread logo. To my sisters, Katharina and Frances, for being my Didis, for your beautiful harmonies, for eating my bread, and for teasing me whenever you get the chance. To my father, Johan, for your encouragement and generous contribution—and for setting an example of writing books.

Thank you to my Oumie Frances, for your deep love and wisdom, and for instilling in all of us a great appreciation of homemade food. To Gogo (Sheelagh), for your spunk and for being a kindred spirit. To my mother-in-law, Melpo, for your kindness and for helping me find my feet in the Greek kitchen. To my late father-in-law, Ioannis, for your generosity and for sharing your recipes and stories from Greece.

Thank you also to Amy Heide (One Organic Farm), Bianca Serfontein (Champagne Valley Stonemill), Kevin Pettersen (Black Fox Flour), and Nico Steyn (Eureka Mills), for answering my long list of questions and for providing insight into the intricacies of wheat farming and milling. And to Bruna Green, for your copious notes and great many pasta recipes—please write a book!

To Melanie Hawken, for building an army of female entrepreneurs. To Nina Morris Lee for offering clarity and purpose when I needed it most. To Caroline Schoenaers, for your mentorship, for teaching me how to delegate, and for reminding me that everything will be okay in the end. To Anna Podrebarac, for falling in love with bread and for taking care of Maggie. To Mary Mammoliti for baking with me on Canadian TV.

To Barbi and Thomas for all your encouragement, advice, and support over the years. To Lydia and Matt Vogelaar for being chosen family.

A heartfelt thank you to all my bread customers and students in South Africa and Canada. Many of the recipes and stories in this book would not exist if it wasn't for you.

And finally, to my husband, Vasili. Thank you for your immense support and patience during the undertaking of this mammoth project. For being there every gruelling step of the way. A joint effort in so many ways!

Further Reading

Vefa's Kitchen by Vefa Alexiadou

Bread, Buns, Cakes and Cookies by Lesley Faull

The Sunset Cookbook of Breads by the editors of Sunset Books and *Sunset* Magazine

The Complete Bread Book by Lorna Walker and Joyce Hughes

Local Breads: Sourdough and Whole-Grain Recipes from Europe's Best Artisan Bakers by Daniel Leader

The Bread Baker's Apprentice: Mastering the Art of Extraordinary Bread by Peter Reinhart

Bread: A Baker's Book of Techniques and Recipes (2nd edition) by Jeffrey Hamelman

The Fundamental Techniques of Classic Bread Baking by the French Culinary Institute

All You Knead is Bread: Over 50 Recipes from Around the World to Bake & Share by Jane Mason

Mooncakes & Milk Bread: Sweet and Savory Recipes Inspired by Chinese Bakeries by Kristina Cho

The South African Culinary Tradition by Renata Coetzee

Knuppeldik aan koningskos compiled by the Pretoria Police Officer's Club's Champion Bakers

Hartskombuis by Boerekos van die Anglo-Boereoorlog tot vandag

Boerekos met 'n twist by Annelien Pienaar

Conversion Chart

VOLUME

Imperial	Metric
⅛ tsp	0.5 mL
¼ tsp	1 mL
½ tsp	2.5 mL
¾ tsp	4 mL
1 tsp	5 mL
½ Tbsp	8 mL
1 Tbsp	15 mL
1½ Tbsp	23 mL
2 Tbsp	30 mL
2½ Tbsp	38 mL
¼ cup	60 mL
⅓ cup	80 mL
½ cup	125 mL
⅔ cup	165 mL
¾ cup	185 mL
1 cup	250 mL
1¼ cups	310 mL
1⅓ cups	330 mL
1½ cups	375 mL
1⅔ cups	415 mL
1¾ cups	435 mL
2 cups/ 1 pint	500 mL
2¼ cups	560 mL
2⅓ cups	580 mL
2½ cups	625 mL
2⅔ cups	665 mL
2¾ cups	690 mL
3 cups	750 mL
3½ cups	875 mL
4 cups	1 L
5 cups	1.25 L
6 cups	1.5 L
8 cups / 2 quarts	2 L
25 cups	6 L

WEIGHT

Imperial	Metric
1 oz	30 g
4 oz	115 g
8 oz	225 g
10 oz	250 g
12 oz	340 g
1 lb (16 oz)	450 g
2 lb	900 g
5 lb	2,250 g

CANS

Imperial	Metric
6 oz	177mL
10 oz	284 mL
11oz	300ml
14 oz	398 mL
16 oz	480 mL
28 oz	796 mL

OVEN TEMPERATURE

Imperial	Metric
200°F	95°C
225°F	105°C
250°F	120°C
275°F	135°C
300°F	150°C
325°F	160°C
350°F	180°C
375°F	190°C
400°F	200°C
425°F	220°C
450°F	230°C

LENGTH/WIDTH

Imperial	Metric
$\frac{1}{12}$ inch	2 mm
⅛ inch	3 mm
⅙ inch	4 mm
¼ inch	6 mm
½ inch	12 mm
¾ inch	2 cm
1 inch	2.5 cm
1½ inches	3.5 cm
2 inches	5 cm
2½ inches	6.5 cm
3 inches	7.5 cm
3½ inches	9 cm
4 inches	10 cm
5 inches	12.5 cm
6 inches	15 cm
7 inches	18 cm
8 inches	20 cm
9 inches	23 cm
10 inches	25 cm

TEMPERATURE

(For oven temperatures, see chart below)

Imperial	Metric
115°F	46°C
150°F	66°C
160°F	71°C
170°F	77°C
180°F	82°C
185°F	85°C
190°F	88°C
200°F	93°C
240°F	116°C
247°F	119°C
250°F	121°C
290°F	143°C
300°F	149°C
350°F	177°C
360°F	182°C
370°F	188°C

US FLUID OUNCES

US fluid ounces	US customary	Metric
¼ oz	½ Tbsp / 1½ tsp	7.5 mL
⅓ oz	2 tsp	10 mL
½ oz	1 Tbsp	15 mL
¾ oz	1½ Tbsp / 4½ tsp	22 mL
1 oz (1 shot)	2 Tbsp	30 mL
1¼ oz	2½ Tbsp	37.5 mL
1½ oz	3 Tbsp	45 mL
2 oz	¼ cup	60 mL
2½ oz	5 Tbsp	75 mL
3 oz	¼ cup + 2 Tbsp	90 mL
3½ oz	¼ cup + 3 Tbsp	105 mL
4 oz	½ cup	125 mL
4½ oz	½ cup + 1 Tbsp	140 mL
5 oz	½ cup + 2 Tbsp	155 mL

Photo credits

Karené Wedekind: vi, 2, 12, 18, 25, 32, 36, 38, 39, 40, 45, 47 (top), 48, 51 (top), 54, 62, 78, 82, 93, 173, 218, 278

Annalize Nel: 4, 43, 47 (bottom), 49, 99, 150

Alon Skuy: 20, 44, 60, 94, 122,

River Makings: ii, iii, 34, 55, 244, 259

Sarah de Roche: 107

Darrin Rigo: 26, 28

Index

A

additives, chemical, 30
ale, dark
  Vollkornbrot (Whole-Kernel Bread), 177–178
  Whole-Grain Seed Loaf, 181–182
all-purpose flour
  about, 21
  The Apprentice Loaf, 138–139
  Beginner's Sourdough, 133–134
  Cold-Fermented Focaccia, 109–110
  Everyday Easy Eating Rye, 135
  Greek Village Bread (Horiatiko Psomi), 143–144
  Mandy's Savoury Cheese & Herb Bread, 225
  Marzipan Stollen, 167–168
  Montreal Bagels, 205–206
  Mosbolletjies (Grape Must Buns), 197
  Oumie's Buttermilk Rusks (Karringmelk Beskuit), 233
  Scones, 222
  Vegan Banana Bread, 227
almonds
  German Hefezopf, 156
  Kitke (Challah), 155–156
  Marzipan Stollen, 167–168
amaranth grains, 22
amasi
  Cornbread (Mieliebrood), 221
  Wholemeal Soda Bread, 223
anise
  Vollkornbrot (Whole-Kernel Bread), 177–178
aniseed
  Greek Tsoureki, 156
  Mosbolletjies (Grape Must Buns), 197
  Raisin Bread with Cinnamon & Aniseed, 163
apples
  Dad's Pancakes (Pannekoek), 215–216
artisan flour, 31
artisan millers, 31
autolyse, mixing, 35–37

B

bacon
  Mandy's Savoury Cheese & Herb Bread, 225
Bagels, Montreal, 205–206
baguette
  Baguette with Poolish, 91–92
  Epi Baguette (Wheat Stalk Baguette or Ear of Wheat Bread), 97
baker's blade, 15, 50
baker's lame, 15, 50
bakery, as an "essential service," 217
baking. *see also* bread baking
  percentages, 84–85
  steps, 34–57
  temperature, 263
  time, 263
  tools, 13–17
  troubleshooting, 260–261
Banana Bread, Vegan, 227
banneton, 15, 42, 49
barley grains
  Vollkornbrot (Whole-Kernel Bread), 177–178
basil
  Mandy's Savoury Cheese & Herb Bread, 225
BBQ
  BBQ Bread (Roosterkoek), 200
  BBQ Toasted Sandwiches (Braaibroodjies), 251
Beaver Tails, 213
beer bread
  Beer Bread (Inspired by Øllebrød), 183–184
  Vollkornbrot (Whole-Kernel Bread), 177–178
  Whole-Grain Seed Loaf, 181–182
bench scraper, 14
Biga, Ciabatta with, 101–102
Black Fox Flour (Canada), 28
blade, baker's, 15, 50
Blyton, Enid, 163
braai (BBQ), 149
Braaibroodjies (BBQ Toasted Sandwiches), 251
brandy
  Marzipan Stollen, 167–168

bread baking. *see also* baking
additions & inclusions, 258
direct method, 61
scheduling baking, 262
stale bread, 245
storing, freezing & defrosting, 259
tools, 50
bread flour. *see also specific types of flour*
about, 20, 21
Baguette with Poolish, 91–92
Ciabatta with Biga, 101–102
Cornbread (Mieliebrood), 221
Epi Baguette (Wheat Stalk Baguette or Ear of Wheat Bread), 97
Hot Cross Buns, 160–161
Koulouria (Greek Sesame Bread Rings), 117–118
Mandy's Savoury Cheese & Herb Bread, 225
Montreal Bagels, 205–206
Pizza Dough, 114–115
Rustic Country Bread with Pâte Fermentée, 87–88
Vegan Banana Bread, 227
bread knife, 17
bread lame, 15
bread pans, 17
bread proofing basket, 14, 42, 49
bread spice
Vollkornbrot (Whole-Kernel Bread), 177–178
Breadcrumbs, 255
breadsticks
Grissini, 237
Kalamata Olive Breadsticks, 89
brotgewürz (bread spice)
Vollkornbrot (Whole-Kernel Bread), 177–178
brown flour, about, 21–22
buckwheat grains, 22
Bunny Chow, 68
buns
BBQ Bread (Roosterkoek), 200
Burger Buns, 198–199
Cinnamon Buns, 164–165
Dombolo (Traditional African Steamed Bread), 210
Hot Cross Buns, 160–161
Laugenbrötchen (German Pretzel Buns), 207–208
Mosbolletjies (Grape Must Buns), 197
Vetkoek (Fried Bread), 211
Burger Buns, 198–199
buttermilk
Cornbread (Mieliebrood), 221
Mandy's Savoury Cheese & Herb Bread, 225
Oumie's Buttermilk Rusks (Karringmelk Beskuit), 233
Scones, 222
Wholemeal Soda Bread, 223

C

cake flour
about, 21
Cornbread (Mieliebrood), 221
Dad's Pancakes (Pannekoek), 215–216
Oumie's Buttermilk Rusks (Karringmelk Beskuit), 233
candied citrus, as an addition, 258
caraway
Vollkornbrot (Whole-Kernel Bread), 177–178
cardamom
Greek Tsoureki, 156
celery
Gogo's Turkey Stuffing, 252
Challah (Kitke), 155–156
Champagne Valley Stonemill (South Africa), 28
cheese, as an addition, 258
chemicals, farming, 29–30
cherries, glace
Marzipan Stollen, 167–168
chilies, as an addition, 258
chocolate, as an addition, 258
chorizo
Mandy's Savoury Cheese & Herb Bread, 225
Ciabatta with Biga, 101–102
cinnamon
Beaver Tails, 213
Cinnamon Buns, 164–165
Dad's Pancakes (Pannekoek), 215–216
Hot Cross Buns, 160–161
Marzipan Stollen, 167–168
Raisin Bread with Cinnamon & Aniseed, 163
Vegan Banana Bread, 227
cloth (couche), 42, 49
cloves
Hot Cross Buns, 160–161
coconut
Oumie's Buttermilk Rusks (Karringmelk Beskuit), 233

cold-fermented breads
  about, 105–107
  final fermentation, 49
  Cold-Fermented Focaccia, 109–110
  Fougasse, 111–112
  Koulouria (Greek Sesame Bread Rings), 117–118
  Pizza Dough, 114–115
  Pot Bread (Potbrood), 199–120
Cologne, Germany, 167
commercial flour-production, 29
consumer information, 28
cooling bread, 57
cooling rack, 17
coriander
  Vollkornbrot (Whole-Kernel Bread), 177–178
Cornbread (Mieliebrood), 221
couche (cloth), 14, 42, 49
country bread. *see* rustic bread
Crackers, Guilty Conscience, 239–240
cream
  Gérard's French Toast, 250
  Scones, 222
currants, as an addition, 258
cutter, dough, 14

D

dark rye flour
  Beer Bread (Inspired by Øllebrød), 183–184
  Everyday Easy Eating Rye, 135
  Whole-Grain Seed Loaf, 181–182
dates
  Vegan Banana Bread, 227
defrosting bread, 259
diastatic malt powder
  Laugenbrötchen (German Pretzel Buns), 207–208
  Montreal Bagels, 205–206
Dinner rolls, 198–199
dip
  Ioannis Kourelos's Skordalia (Greek Garlic & Bread Dip), 247
direct method, 61
Dombolo (Traditional African Steamed Bread), 210
doppio zero flour
  Bruna's Egg Pasta, 241–242
dough
  Pizza Dough, 114–115
  scrapers, 13
  straight, 61
  troubleshooting, 260–261
Dutch oven, 17, 53

E

Easter Bread, Italian, 156
Eat Your Heart Out restaurant, 201
eating bread, 57
egg wash
  Hot Cross Buns, 160–161
  Kitke (Challah), 155–156
  Milk Bread, 157–158
eggs
  Bruna's Egg Pasta, 241–242
  Gérard's French Toast, 250
  Mandy's Savoury Cheese & Herb Bread, 225
  Oumie's Buttermilk Rusks (Karringmelk Beskuit), 233
einkorn flour, about, 22
emmer flour, about, 22
enriched flour, 29
Epi Baguette (Wheat Stalk Baguette or Ear of Wheat Bread), 97
Eureka Mills (South Africa), 28
Everything Bagel Seasoning
  Guilty Conscience Crackers, 239–240
  Montreal Bagels, 205–206

F

The Famous Five (Blyton), 163
Farm Inn, 3
farming chemicals, 29–30
farming wheat, 27–31
farro grains
  Vollkornbrot (Whole-Kernel Bread), 177–178
  Whole-Grain Seed Loaf, 181–182
fennel seeds
  Everyday Easy Eating Rye, 135
  Vollkornbrot (Whole-Kernel Bread), 177–178
fermentation. *see also* pre-fermentation
  bulk, 40
  cold, 105–107
  final, 49
  gluten structure, 41
  poolish pre-ferment, 239–240
  salt, 24
  time, 263
  yeast, 24
Flatbread, Rustic, 75
flax seed
  Vollkornbrot (Whole-Kernel Bread), 177–178

flour. *see also specific types of flour*
baker's percentages, 84–85
commercial production, 29
enrichment, 29
shaker, 14
Focaccia, Cold-Fermented, 109–110
fortification, flour, 29
Fougasse, 111–112
Frances (author's sister), 2, 169
freezing bread, 57, 259
French Toast, Gérard's, 250
fried bread
Beaver Tails, 213
Berliner, 212
Fried Dough Variations, 212–213
Vetkoek (Fried Bread), 211

G

garlic
as an addition, 258
Cold-Fermented Focaccia, 109–110
Fougasse, 111–112
Ioannis Kourelos's Skordalia (Greek Garlic & Bread Dip), 247
Mama Mou's Garlic Bread, 249
German Hefezopf, 156
German Pretzel Buns (Laugenbrötchen), 207–208
gluten
about, 20, 21, 172
autolyse, 37
shaping, 42
stretch and fold, 40–41
structure, 20, 41
water and, 23
wheat hardness, 30
yeast and, 24
GMOs, 30
Gogo's Turkey Stuffing, 252
Government Loaf (Soft White Sandwich Bread), 67–68
grains, as an addition, 258
grains soaking, 175
grape juice
Mosbolletjies (Grape Must Buns), 197
Grape Must Buns (Mosbolletjies), 197
Greek Garlic & Bread Dip (Ioannis Kourelos's Skordalia), 247
Greek Sesame Bread Rings (Koulouria), 117–118
Greek Tsoureki, 156
Greek Village Bread (Horiatiko Psomi), 143–144
Greek yogurt
Cornbread (Mieliebrood), 221
Mandy's Savoury Cheese & Herb Bread, 225
Scones, 222
Sesame seed topping, 75
Green, Bruna (née Perotti), 241–242

H

halloumi
Mandy's Savoury Cheese & Herb Bread, 225
Hefezopf, German, 156
herbs, as an addition, 258
heritage wheat flours, about, 22
high protein bread flour
about, 20
Bruna's Egg Pasta, 241–242
Montreal Bagels, 205–206
home bakery, 103
honey
Greek Village Bread (Horiatiko Psomi), 143–144
Kitke (Challah), 155–156
Koulouria (Greek Sesame Bread Rings), 117–118
Montreal Bagels, 205–206
Mosbolletjies (Grape Must Buns), 197
Oat & Honey Loaf, 186–187
Old-Fashioned Cottage Loaf with Spelt, 65
The 33% Loaf, 185
Horiatiko Psomi (Greek Village Bread), 143–144
Hot Dog rolls, 198–199
hydration, 23–24, 40, 42

I

icing
Cinnamon Buns, 164–165
ingredients
mixing, 39
sourcing, 34
Italian Easter Bread, 156

J

jalapeños
as an addition, 258
Mandy's Savoury Cheese & Herb Bread, 225
jam
Berliner, 212
Johan (author's father), 2

K

Kalamata Olive Breadsticks, 89
Kamut flour, about, 22
Karringmelk Beskuit (Oumie's Buttermilk Rusks), 233
Kassa (Little Addis restaurant), 201
Katharina (author's sister), 2, 169
kefir
  Wholemeal Soda Bread, 223
Kevin (author's stepfather), 6, 169
kitchen scales, 13
Kitke (Challah), 155–156
kneading, 39
knife, bread, 17
Koulouria (Greek Sesame Bread Rings), 117–118
Kourelos, Ioannis, 143, 247

L

lame, baker's, 15, 50
Laugenbrötchen (German Pretzel Buns), 207–208
lemon
  Dad's Pancakes (Pannekoek), 215–216
  Marzipan Stollen, 167–168
  Ukrainian Paska Bread, 156
levain, 7, 103, 128, 137
Little Addis restaurant, 201

M

Maastricht, the Netherlands, 135
Maboneng bakery, 9, 94, 121, 201
Maggie (the sourdough levain), 128
mahleb
  Greek Tsoureki, 156
mahlepi
  Greek Tsoureki, 156
maize meal
  Cornbread (Mieliebrood), 221
Makoto, Washington, 94, 121, 201
Mama Clementina, 201
maple syrup
  Oat & Honey Loaf, 186–187
  The 33% Loaf, 185
mastic
  Greek Tsoureki, 156
mastiha
  Greek Tsoureki, 156
Melpo (author's mom-in-law), 3
Michaletos, Constantine Alexander, 2
Michaletos, Paradeisios, 1
Mieliebrood (Cornbread), 221
miixing, direct method, 61
milk
  Dad's Pancakes (Pannekoek), 215–216
  Greek Village Bread (Horiatiko Psomi), 143–144
  Hot Cross Buns, 160–161
  Marzipan Stollen, 167–168
  Mosbolletjies (Grape Must Buns), 197
  Oat & Honey Loaf, 186–187
  Pizza Dough, 114–115
  Scones, 222
  Simple Milk Loaf, 77
milling wheat, 27–31
mint
  Mandy's Savoury Cheese & Herb Bread, 225
mise en place, 38
mixing bowls, 13
mixing ingredients, 39
Montreal Bagels, 205–206
Mosbolletjies (Grape Must Buns), 197

N

Nicholas Day festival, 153
Nutella
  Dad's Pancakes (Pannekoek), 215–216
nuts
  as an addition, 258
  Kitke (Challah), 155–156
  Marzipan Stollen, 167–168
  Vegan Banana Bread, 227

O

oats
  Oat & Honey Loaf, 186–187
  Vollkornbrot (Whole-Kernel Bread), 177–178
  Whole-Grain Seed Loaf, 181–182
olives
  as an addition, 258
  Fougasse, 111–112
  Kalamata Olive Breadsticks, 89
  Mandy's Savoury Cheese & Herb Bread, 225
One Organic Farm (Canada), 28
onions
  BBQ Toasted Sandwiches (Braaibroodjies), 251
  Gogo's Turkey Stuffing, 252

orange
  Greek Tsoureki, 156
  Italian Easter Bread, 156
  Marzipan Stollen, 157–168
  Ukrainian Paska Bread, 156
organic flours, 30
Oumie's Buttermilk Rusks (Karringmelk Beskuit), 233
oven-safe pot, 17

P

pan, pullman, 17
Pancakes (Pannekoek), Dad's, 215–216
pans, bread, 17
parsley
  Mama Mou's Garlic Bread, 249
Pasta, Bruna's Egg, 241–242
Pâte Fermentée, Rustic Country Bread with, 87–88
peel
  as an addition, 258
  Marzipan Stollen, 167–168
pepperoni
  Mandy's Savoury Cheese & Herb Bread, 225
peppers, jalapeños
  as an addition, 258
  Mandy's Savoury Cheese & Herb Bread, 225
percentages
  baker's, 84–85
Perotti, Clara, 241–242
perservatives, 29
petimez/pekmezi
  Koulouria (Greek Sesame Bread Rings), 117–118
Pita Pockets & Gyro Pita Wraps, 191–192
Pizza Dough, 114–115
poolish
  about, 83
  Baguette with Poolish, 91–92
  Pre-ferment, 239–240
poppy seeds
  Guilty Conscience Crackers, 239–240
  Kitke (Challah), 155–156
  Montreal Bagels, 205–206
pork
  Gogo's Turkey Stuffing, 252
pot, oven-safe, 17
potato
  Ioannis Kourelos's Skordalia (Greek Garlic & Bread Dip), 247
pre-fermentation
  about, 35, 79, 81, 83
  baker's percentages, 84–85
pre-fermented breads
  Baguette with Poolish, 91–92
  Ciabatta with Biga, 101–102
  Epi Baguette (Wheat Stalk Baguette or Ear of Wheat Bread), 97
  Rustic Country Bread with Pâte Fermentée, 87–88
Pretzel Buns, German (Laugenbrötchen), 207–208
proofing
  cloth (couche), 42, 49
  final, 49
  scoring and, 50
  troubleshooting, 260–261
pullman pan, 17, 53
pumpkin seeds
  Vollkornbrot (Whole-Kernel Bread), 177–178
Puratos company, 30

Q

quick breads
  about, 219
  Cornbread (Mieliebrood), 221
quinoa grains, 22

R

raisins
  as an addition, 258
  Hot Cross Buns, 160–161
  Mandy's Savoury Cheese & Herb Bread, 225
  Marzipan Stollen, 167–168
  Raisin Bread with Cinnamon & Aniseed, 163
ratios
  baker's percentages, 84–85
ratios, water, 23–24
Real Bread Campaign, 28
Red Fife flour, about, 22
red spring wheat, 30
red winter wheat, 30
rising, troubleshooting, 260–261
roasting pan, 53
rolls
  BBQ Bread (Roosterkoek), 200
  Dinner Rolls, Burger Buns & Hot Dog Rolls, 198–199
  Hot Dog rolls, 198–199
  Portuguese Rolls (Papo Secos), 195

rooibos tea
    Marzipan Stollen, 167–168
Roome, Sheelagh (née Coalter), 252
Roosterkoek (BBQ Bread), 200
rosemary
    Cold-Fermented Focaccia, 109–110
    Guilty Conscience Crackers, 239–240
Rubard, Gérard, 7, 137, 138–139, 141, 149, 250
rum
    Marzipan Stollen, 167–168
rusks
    about, 230–231
    Bread Rusks, 235
    Oumie's Buttermilk Rusks (Karringmelk Beskuit), 233
rustic bread
    Rustic Country Bread with Pâte Fermentée, 87–88
    Rustic Country Loaf, 73
    Rustic Flatbreads, 75
rye bread
    about, 171–173, 175
    Beer Bread (Inspired by Øllebrød), 183–184
    Vollkornbrot (Whole-Kernel Bread), 177–178
    Whole-Grain Seed Loaf, 181–182
rye flour
    about, 22
    Everyday Easy Eating Rye, 135
    Rustic Country Bread with Pâte Fermentée, 87–88
    The 33% Loaf, 185

S

sage
    Gogo's Turkey Stuffing, 252
salt
    about, 24
    baker's percentages, 84–85
sandwich bread
    Brown Sandwich Bread, 71
    Government Loaf (Soft White Sandwich Bread), 67–68
    Sourdough Sandwich Bread, 147–148
sandwiches
    BBQ Toasted Sandwiches (Braaibroodjies), 251
sausage
    Gogo's Turkey Stuffing, 252
    Mandy's Savoury Cheese & Herb Bread, 225
savoury bread
    Mandy's Savoury Cheese & Herb Bread, 225
scales, kitchen, 13
scheduling baking, 262
schmalz
    Laugenbrötchen (German Pretzel Buns), 207–208
Scones, 222
scoring, 50
    proofing and, 50
scraper, bench, 14
scrapers, dough, 13
The Secret Seven (Blyton), 163
seeds, as an addition, 258
semolina flour
    about, 22
    Greek Village Bread (Horiatiko Psomi), 143–144
sesame seeds
    Grissini, 237
    Guilty Conscience Crackers, 239–240
    Kitke (Challah), 155–156
    Koulouria (Greek Sesame Bread Rings), 117–118
    Montreal Bagels, 205–206
    Sesame seed topping, 75
    Vollkornbrot (Whole-Kernel Bread), 177–178
shaker, flour, 14
Sha'p Braai restaurant, 201
shaping and pre-shaping, 46, 47
soaking grains, 175
Soda Bread, Wholemeal, 223
sorghum grains, 22
sourdough baking
    about, 123–126
    baker's percentages, 84–85
    levain, 7, 103, 128, 137
    Make Your Own Sourdough Culture, 130–131
    ratios, 127
    starters, 35–37, 127–128
sourdough bread
    The Apprentice Loaf, 138–139
    Beginner's Sourdough, 133–134
    Everyday Easy Eating Rye, 135
    Gérard's Sourdough (Pain au Levain), 141–142
    Greek Village Bread (Horiatiko Psomi), 143–144
    Guilty Conscience Crackers, 239–240
    Pain au Levain aka (Traditional French Sourdough), 137
    Sourdough Sandwich Bread, 147–148
    The 33% Loaf, 185
    Vollkornbrot (Whole-Kernel Bread), 177–178

spelt flour
  The Apprentice Loaf, 138–139
  Beer Bread (Inspired by Øllebrød), 183–184
  Guilty Conscience Crackers, 239–240
  Old-Fashioned Cottage Loaf with Spelt, 65
  Vegan Banana Bread, 227
spelt grains
  Vollkornbrot (Whole-Kernel Bread), 177–178
  Whole-Grain Seed Loaf, 181–182
spices. as an addition, 258
spray bottle, 17, 54
spring onions
  Mandy's Savoury Cheese & Herb Bread, 225
stale bread, 245
steam baking, 53–54
steamed bread
  Dombolo (Traditional African Steamed Bread), 210
stollen
  Marzipan Stollen, 167–168
Stollen, Marzipan, 167–168
stone milling, 30
storing bread, 57, 259
straight dough, 61
stretch and fold, 39, 40, 41
Stuffing, Gogo's Turkey, 252
Stutenkerl, 153
sugar moderation, 158
sultanas
  as an addition, 258
  Hot Cross Buns, 160–161
  Marzipan Stollen, 167–168
sun-dried tomatoes
  as an addition, 258
  Mandy's Savoury Cheese & Herb Bread, 225
sunflower seeds
  Vollkornbrot (Whole-Kernel Bread), 177–178
  Whole-Grain Seed Loaf, 181–182
sweet and enriched breads
  about, 153
  German Hefezopf, 156
  Greek Tsoureki, 156
  Hot Cross Buns, 160–161
  Italian Easter Bread, 156
  Kitke (Challah), 155–156
  Marzipan Stollen, 167–168
  Milk Bread, 157–158
  Raisin Bread with Cinnamon & Aniseed, 163
  Ukrainian Paska Bread, 156

T

tangzhong
  Milk Bread, 157–158
teff grains, 22
temperature, oven, 54, 263
Theodora (author's mother), 2, 6, 249
thyme
  Fougasse, 111–112
  Gogo's Turkey Stuffing, 252
tomatoes
  BBQ Toasted Sandwiches (Braaibroodjies), 251
tools, 13–17, 50
topping
  Cold-Fermented Focaccia, 109–110
  Fougasse, 111–112
  Kitke (Challah), 155–156
  Koulouria (Greek Sesame Bread Rings), 117–118
  Olive Oil and záatar topping, 75
  Rustic Flatbreads, 75
  Sesame seed topping, 75
Tosi, Christina, 151
troubleshooting, 260–261

V

vanilla
  Marzipan Stollen, 167–168
Vasili (author's husband), 3, 121
Vegan Banana Bread, 227
Vermont apprenticeship, 7
Vetkoek (Fried Bread), 211
Vollkornbrot (Whole-Kernel Bread), 177–178

W

water
  about, 23
  adjusting, 263
  baker's percentages, 84–85
  hydration, 23–24, 40, 42
  ratio, 23–24
Weckmann, 153
wheat berries, 30, 31
wheat bran
  about, 29
  Oumie's Buttermilk Rusks (Karringmelk Beskuit), 233
wheat farming and milling, 27–31
wheat flour, about, 20

white bread flour
- The Apprentice Loaf, 138–139
- Beer Bread (Inspired by Øllebrød), 183–184
- Beginner's Sourdough, 133–134
- Cold-Fermented Focaccia, 109–110
- Everyday Easy Eating Rye, 135
- Greek Village Bread (Horiatiko Psomi), 143–144
- Kitke (Challah), 155–156
- Laugenbrötchen (German Pretzel Buns), 207–208
- Marzipan Stollen, 167–168
- Milk Bread, 157–158
- Oat & Honey Loaf, 186–187
- Rustic Country Bread with Pâte Fermentée, 87–88
- The 33% Loaf, 185
- Whole-Grain Seed Loaf, 181–182

white flour
- Brown Sandwich Bread, 71
- Government Loaf (Soft White Sandwich Bread), 67–68
- Rustic Country Bread with Pâte Fermentée, 87–88
- Rustic Country Loaf, 73
- Simple Milk Loaf, 77

whole-grain bread
- about, 175
- Beer Bread (Inspired by Øllebrød), 183–184
- Oat & Honey Loaf, 186–187
- The 33% Loaf, 185
- Vollkornbrot (Whole-Kernel Bread), 177–178
- Whole-Grain Seed Loaf, 181–182

whole-grain flour. *see* whole wheat flour

whole wheat flour
- about, 21–22
- Brown Sandwich Bread, 71
- Guilty Conscience Crackers, 239–240
- Oat & Honey Loaf, 186–187
- Old-Fashioned Cottage Loaf with Spelt, 65
- The 33% Loaf, 185
- Wholemeal Soda Bread, 223

wholemeal. *see* whole-grain bread; whole wheat flour

Wraps, Pita Pockets & Gyro Pita, 191–192

Y

yeast
- about, 24
- baker's percentages, 84–85
- Baguette with Poolish, 91–92
- Brown Sandwich Bread, 71
- Government Loaf (Soft White Sandwich Bread), 67–68
- Old-Fashioned Cottage Loaf with Spelt, 65
- Rustic Country Bread with Pâte Fermentée, 87–88
- Rustic Country Loaf, 73
- Simple Milk Loaf, 77

yogurt
- Sesame seed topping, 75
- Wholemeal Soda Bread, 223

Z

za'atar, 75